Your
College Faith

OWN IT!

Your
College Faith
OWN IT!

Matt and Colleen Swaim

Liguori
LIGUORI, MISSOURI

Imprimi Potest:
Harry Grile, CSsR, Provincial
Denver Province, The Redemptorists

Published by Liguori Publications
Liguori, Missouri 63057

To order, call 800-325-9521
www.liguori.org

Cataloging-in-Publication Data on file with the Library of Congress.

pISBN: 978-0-7648-2192-9
eISBN: 978-0-7648-2310-7

Excerpts from English translation of the *Catechism of the Catholic Church* for the United States of America © 1994, United States Catholic Conference, Inc.—*Libreria Editrice Vaticana*; English translation of the *Catechism of the Catholic Church: Modifications from the Editio Typica* © 1997, United States Catholic Conference, Inc.—*Libreria Editrice Vaticana*.

Unless otherwise noted, Scripture quotations are from *New Revised Standard Version Bible*, copyright © 1989 National Council of the Churches of Christ in the United States of America. Used by permission. All rights reserved.

Excerpts from Vatican documents used with permission. Copyright © Libreria Editrice Vaticana.

G. K. Chesterton excerpts from *The Collected Works of G. K. Chesterton*, Vols. 32 and 35, © 1989 and 1990. All rights reserved. Used by permission of Ignatius Press, San Francisco, CA.

Excerpts from the English translation of *The General Instruction of the Roman Missal* from *The Roman Missal* © 2010, International Commission on English in the Liturgy Corporation. All rights reserved.

Compliant with *The Roman Missal*, third edition.

Liguori Publications, a nonprofit corporation, is an apostolate of The Redemptorists. To learn more about The Redemptorists, visit Redemptorists.com.

Printed in the United States of America
17 16 15 14 13 / 5 4 3 2 1
First Edition

Contents

Foreword

I was one of a vanishing breed. Raised Catholic, I stopped practicing my faith in college, only to return because of friends who cared enough to hold my hand and lead me back. I am a revert.

Stories like my own are becoming more and more rare. Every year a growing number of Catholics stop practicing their faith and never return. College can still be a place of education and maturation, but for most young adults raised Catholic, it is now the place where they lose their faith. I should know, having worked with college students in Catholic campus ministry for over a decade.

The numbers are staggering. Self-identified Catholic college-aged adults attend Mass at the lowest percentage of any generation in history (nearly single-digit percentage). For a good many years, college has been a minefield of dangers: alcohol, drugs, sex outside of marriage, pornography, cheating, and so forth. Into this poisonous mixture, our culture has added philosophies that make things even worse:

Relativism—Truth is relative to a person, belief, or situation.

Utilitarianism—The best course of action is the one that maximizes happiness and reduces suffering.

Materialism—Our ultimate happiness is found in things, and there is no spiritual reality.

We Catholics have not responded well to these issues. Too long we have relied on the Catholic culture from past generations to help raise children in the faith. The results show that relying merely on this Catholic culture is not working anymore. We need deeper prayer, renewed efforts of reaching out to others, and a strong personal devotion to Christ.

The answers to staying Catholic in college (and growing in virtue, holiness, and maturity in the process) will not be found in another program. Nor will it be found in waiting for the right document from the Pope. It is found in individuals who make good decisions, are willing to get dirty in the trenches, and do the hard work of reaching out to the lost, proclaiming the Gospel to all, investing ourselves in those who want to be followers of Christ (and teaching them what that means), teaching prayer, and then sending them out to do the same. Chances are, you are one of those who will need some help from others. Don't be shy in seeking out others who will nourish your faith.

The book you hold has great wisdom and practical advice. I can guarantee if you follow the lead of Matt and Colleen, you will be one who leaves college as a practicing Catholic, who has grown in the faith and taken it on as your own. You might even be the next Catholic evangelist who helps non-practicing Catholics, like myself in college, come back to the faith.

MARCEL LEJEUNE
ASSISTANT DIRECTOR OF CAMPUS MINISTRY
ST. MARY'S CATHOLIC CENTER
TEXAS A&M UNIVERSITY

Introduction

Are you a high school graduate preparing to go to a state or private institution? Perhaps you are a senior in college who has just begun to connect with your faith. And maybe you have decided to stay at home while attending your local community college. Regardless of your college context, this book is intended to assist you in keeping the candle of faith well lit through your collegiate years.

Whether you've been home-schooled, gone to Catholic school, attended a public school, or experienced a combination of all the above, no educational experience to this point can fully prepare you for what you'll experience or already have experienced the first day you set foot on the campus of the undergraduate institution of your choice.

No matter what background you come from, if you're a practicing Catholic, prepare to be scandalized on your first weekend as a myriad of worldviews assault your senses. After your first few days at college, you may be tempted to think one of two things: either you're the only person on campus with good sense or everything you've been told about faith and the universe is a lie and you need to start from scratch. Neither of these approaches will get to the heart of the concerns you face as a Catholic trying to live your faith on campus. In addition to that, prepare to have your daily routine upended, your social landscape rototilled, and your concept of your own personal identity revolutionized.

College presents a totally different universe than the one you experienced in high school. That doesn't mean you have to become a totally different person than you were in high school; it just means you're continuing to develop your understanding of what it means to be a Catholic Christian as a young adult. Just because the simplified forms about Christ and his Church that you believed as a third-grader seem overly basic for the situations you face in college doesn't mean Jesus is no longer relevant once you cruise past your confirmation and into your collegiate career.

If something is true, *really* true, it'll maintain its truthfulness as well when applied to your lived scholastic situation: through middle school, high school, and even into the academic discipline you choose for your own personal collegiate path. Science, literature, philosophy, history—our Catholic faith touches each of these subjects, and it's important to be grounded in your faith so that when it's challenged in or outside the classroom, you'll be equipped to handle those challenges.

You may be tempted to draw away from regular Mass attendance by atheists, Protestants, or even Catholics who don't think the sacraments are all that important. However, you'll have to assert yourself no matter who tempts you, because, as Jesus says in John 15:4, "Abide in me as I abide in you. Just as the branch cannot bear fruit by itself unless it abides in the vine, neither can you unless you abide in me." You may not be connected to your home parish like you were before college, but don't let that keep you from being connected to the Church while you're at college.

You'll face no shortage of challenges to living your Catholic faith as you transition into life as an undergraduate. Our hope is that this book—while not claiming to be a *be-all and end-all* guide to living your faith—will at least get you to thinking about the basic challenges to your Catholicism that you'll face as a student and guide you toward resources that can help you stay connected to Christ and his Church.

How to Use This Book

As we take a look at some of the challenges you'll face or are already facing as a college student, our goal is to provide you with reflections you can return to when these challenges occur. Each chapter is structured interactively so that you can add your own thoughts as you read.

After beginning with a quote from Scripture or a papal document and a brief overview of each area of campus life, you'll read about some scenarios you might encounter in the classroom, the dorm room, or in social settings. Take some time to think through these scenarios in advance so that when you're confronted with them in the moment, you won't be caught off-guard.

When you've finished reading about why each aspect of college life brought up in this book is important, you'll be inspired by "alumni profiles" or stories of saints who struggled as you may with everything from keeping balance in the midst of a busy schedule to withstanding the pressure to go against your conscience in a tempting situation. The less regrets you have about the way you conduct yourself in college, the better!

Toward the end of each chapter, you'll see what the *Catechism of the Catholic Church* has to say about the subject matter of that particular chapter. After that, you'll find a series of practical ways to act on your faith in a campus setting, followed by a list of other books to explore if you want to delve deeper into a particular issue. Finally, you'll find prayers that you can visit repeatedly in the course of your collegiate career.

Remember, this book is designed to be interactive—you're encouraged to write down your own thoughts and experiences as you see fit. Then perhaps years from now, you'll be able to flip back through these pages and revisit some of the formative landmarks in your spiritual life.

1

Own It! Your Faith as Authentically Yours

Hold to the standard of sound teaching that you have heard from me, in the faith and love that are in Christ Jesus. Guard the good treasure entrusted to you, with the help of the Holy Spirit living in us.

---

2 TIMOTHY 1:13–14

Technically speaking, nobody is born Catholic, though some of us came close, having been baptized as infants. Others of us perhaps came into the Church individually or with our families later on in our childhood or school-age years. Under the guidance of parents, grandparents, or Catholic-school teachers, you probably attended classes where you learned some of the nuts and bolts of the faith and may even have been active in your parish youth ministry along the way. All the work you and those who love you have done to help your faith take root in your life has been preparing you for the moment when you finally leave the nest, take off the training wheels, and begin to flourish in the Church as a young adult.

College provides many gifts and opportunities when it comes to making your faith your own. Now it's your turn to take the initiative to go to Mass and confession, your turn to decide to read materials and engage in activities that further your spiritual growth, and your turn to become the kind of person who honors Christ with your life when nobody's looking. That includes the tough task of scrutinizing what is valued and mainstream in contemporary life and figuring out if it truly meshes with who you are as a Catholic young adult. Maturing in your Catholic faith is a challenging though ultimately exciting process as you move to a whole new level in your relationship with God.

What name did you take at your confirmation? Which saint does it honor? How can you further emulate his or her life while in college?

_____

_____

_____

_____

_____

Why It's Important to Take This Chapter Seriously

Throughout your life, you've no doubt encountered opinions that were indifferent or even hostile to your Catholic faith. These challenges may have come from the media, friends at school, or even family members such as those Catholics who no longer practice their faith. Through social media, exposure to a myriad of worldviews is becoming more and more possible at earlier ages, and college tends to be the ultimate testing ground in this regard. Understanding how people object to Catholicism in unique and varied ways will help you to better understand why you believe what you believe. It's time for you to do the leg work and figure out why Catholicism offers more than the faith of Buddhists, nondenominational Protestants, Mormons, or even agnostics. Like many of your college subjects, you might have to do some critical thinking here. And it's certainly necessary to keep praying through moments of doubt or confusion.

In college, chances are you'll meet in person for the first time people from belief systems you've previously only read about. You'll have questions for them, just as they'll surely have questions for you. Some of their questions are bound to make you uncomfortable, especially if you're not sure how to answer them. Just like your parents may have grown more deeply in their faith as they researched answers to difficult questions about the faith that you asked as a young child, you can use these questions from friends as an opportunity to grow in your own faith as you try to explain to others what it means to be a Catholic. After all, how can you defend something you don't understand, or more important, how can you share your faith if you're not sure why you believe in the first place?

As you begin to take full ownership of your Catholic faith, it may be helpful to start at the beginning:

Where did your Catholic faith come from? Was it from your parents? Your grandparents?

_____

_____

_____

_____

_____

_____

Can you remember a point in your childhood when you were sure God existed? What was it that convinced you then?

_____

_____

_____

_____

_____

_____

Between birth and college, almost everyone has resisted going to church one Sunday or another. If you were reluctant to go to Mass at some point in your life, what was the source of that reluctance?

_____

_____

_____

_____

Has your experience of high school made you more or less convinced that God exists and loves you?

_____

_____

_____

_____

It's time to begin examining exactly why you're Catholic, especially since sooner or later someone is going to question you about it. Have you stayed Catholic because of a nagging relative or because you deeply believe in the importance of meeting Jesus regularly in the Eucharist? Why Catholicism, and what does this identity mean for you? With thousands of Christian denominations to choose from, why would you want to share the faith of your ancestors any more than you'd want to share their interest in music? If you've ever considered being something besides Catholic, what was it and why? All of these and more are questions Catholics interested in taking ownership of their faith need to be asking themselves as they grow in Christian maturity. And stepping onto a college campus and out from under the umbrella of your parents provides a chance to address these questions from a different angle, allowing you to decipher what you believe and why.

Perhaps some aspects of the faith seem as natural to you as breathing—things like the importance of baptism, devotion to Mary, the necessity of the priesthood, and the observance of Lent. But these ideas may seem totally foreign to people from other faith backgrounds, whether they be new friends, roommates, professors, or acquaintances. Take some time to explore the things that obviously set Catholicism apart from other worldviews. Try to understand why the Church places an emphasis on these aspects of our faith that people of other faiths don't seem to think are important at all, or perhaps even find offensive about Catholicism.

If you attend a Catholic college or university, you probably assume that deepening your faith will come naturally—that opportunities for growth will be as common and mainstream as a classmate planning her fantasy wedding or a hallmate streaming online movies. You probably also assume you'll be fairly free of challenges to your Catholic beliefs. The fact is, you may have to work as hard or harder at a Catholic university than you would at a secular college to avoid taking the gift of your faith for granted and sinking into a malaise. At secular colleges, Christian colleges, and even many specifically Catholic colleges, skeptical postmodernist theory—which puts forth the idea that absolute truth doesn't exist and isn't even possible—is far too prevalent. As such, don't take for granted that your professors are right just because they are teaching at a reputable university or have several letters behind their name. It is possible to be highly intelligent and totally wrong. However, this does not mean you should not consider what they are teaching as reputable. Though they could be wrong, sometimes it takes discernment in thought and prayer to assimilate some information.

Furthermore, we humans like to do our own thing and stay comfortable. However, seeking out higher truths as a student means not only reaching toward the meaning of eternity with your heart, soul, mind, and strength but also living a life consistent with the meaning of the eternal truths that you will hopefully come to know and love in new ways as a maturing Catholic. The work of *owning* your college faith takes time, but God is with you and accompanies you through these struggles. God wants you to understand the gift of faith you received at baptism.

Many times, people's objections to Catholicism will have more to do with the failings of those who profess the Catholic faith rather than a misunderstanding of doctrine. If someone were to ask you how you could be part of a Church that has seen some of its priests exposed as sexual child abusers, what would you say? If someone asked why you'd want to align yourself with the same institution that arrested a scientist like Galileo, led inquisitions in Rome and Spain, and engaged in the Crusades, how would you respond? Perhaps the most antagonistic questions you'll face won't come from atheists, agnostics, or Protestant Christians. Rather, they may come from those who were raised Catholic but had a series of bad experiences with clergy and fellow Catholics or who found the moral teachings of the Church, particularly on issues of sexuality, challenging. If you are struggling with the same issues as they are, what would keep you Catholic?

Write down one objection someone you know has put forth as a reason they could never be Catholic.

_____

_____

_____

_____

_____

Put aside a chunk of time this week to seek out answers to that question from a trusted source, such as the *Catechism of the Catholic Church*, YOUCAT, or a faithful Catholic priest or other mentor.

In addition to the challenging questions others will have about your faith, you may have some challenging questions of your own—perhaps questions as big as how can we even be sure that God exists. Some outside the Church criticize Catholics as a bunch of unquestioning automatons of the pope, an army of robotic simpletons just waiting for orders and afraid to think for themselves.

A survey of the lives and teachings of some of the doctors of the Church shows that we as Catholics regard those great minds that asked the hardest questions to be some of our proudest family members in the communion of saints. This includes people like Saint Augustine, the brilliant writer and orator, who tried out a number of different philosophies and lifestyles before finally arriving at the conclusion that Catholicism was the one true faith. Saint Thérèse of Lisieux was a Carmelite nun who desperately desired to be a missionary but was too weak to go to foreign lands. Her spirituality of the *little way* has inspired many and earned her the title of doctor of the Church. Saint Thomas Aquinas wrote the *Summa Theologiae,* a massive collection of objections to Catholic belief wherein he grants his opponents massive benefit of the doubt and uses reason to argue and prove the Church's theological perspective.

And Blessed John Henry Newman, after whom the Newman Centers on many college campuses are named, was part of an intellectual movement that sought to prove the historical validity of the schismatic Church of England when he came to the conclusion that Catholicism was the only faith consistent with the one founded by Jesus on the rock of Saint Peter. It was Newman, by the way, who said, "Ten thousand difficulties do not make one doubt." According to Newman, asking the toughest questions about the Church in a spirit of charity is not an act of defiance, but an act of love. You will never be able to own your faith until you explore the difficult questions for yourself and find the explanations that resonate with you personally in your spiritual walk as a Catholic.

This chapter led off with a verse from Saint Paul's Second Letter to Saint Timothy, where he encourages Timothy to carefully "guard the good treasure entrusted to you." Paul and Timothy had a special relationship. Paul knew both Timothy's mother and grandmother to be faithful Christians and was aware of the lengths to which they had gone to ensure that Timothy had a solid foundation of faith. We know their efforts paid off, because Paul's letters to Timothy in the New Testament are among what we refer to as the "pastoral Epistles," letters Paul wrote to a couple of the Church's early bishops, teaching them how to conduct themselves as they went about instructing the faithful. As Saint Paul's letters indicate, Timothy was a young man when he became the first bishop of Ephesus, which should encourage you as a college student to know that you don't have to be advanced in years to be a Christian leader. But something else can be learned from this relationship between Paul and Timothy. In both of his letters, Paul uses fatherly language when referring to Timothy, calling him "my loyal child in the faith" (1 Timothy 1:2) and "my beloved child" (2 Timothy 1:2), even though there was no biological relationship between these two men.

This underscores the importance of finding a mentor in the faith. This could be someone with whom you formally meet for spiritual direction or instruction, but it also means seeking out fellow Catholic classmates who may be a step ahead of you when it comes to Christian maturity. At college, you'll find Catholic students who are at your level in regard to the love and knowledge of their faith, as well as those who are at different points in their spiritual journey, both ahead of you and behind you. This is why it's important to plug in to some kind of Catholic community on campus such as a Newman Center located on many public universities or the campus ministry provided by Catholic universities.

Additionally, sometimes you will find outreach groups such as the Fellowship of Catholic University Students (FOCUS) or St. Paul's Outreach to help you revitalize your faith. Through these channels you will not only find adult campus-ministry leaders who are willing to help you make your faith your own, but also fellow Catholic students who have walked the path you're trying to walk and who were likely in the same place as you not so long ago. These are the people you want to meet with at coffeehouses and campus hangouts to dig more deeply into questions of faith. When you get hit with a challenge to the faith that you don't know how to answer, you will likely encounter the living Church through these people, because odds are they've been approached with the same challenges. These are the same people who will encourage you to join them for Mass on Sundays and who are trying to live out the Church's moral teaching on a campus full of temptations. Developing a community of fellow pilgrims along the path to spiritual maturity is an excellent way to guard and strengthen your Catholic faith as you seek truth both within as well as outside the normal educational structures.

Who mentored you in the faith throughout high school? Did he or she do a good job? Explain.

_____

_____

_____

_____

_____

Growing up, you probably knew people who stopped going to church in high school, perhaps even earlier. In college, too, you'll likely see Catholics who decide not to go to church, at least for a while. Research shows that people stop going to Mass in college less out of disagreement with Church teaching than out of getting caught up in the whirlwind of distractions that campus life provides. In the whirlwind of college adventures, Mass sometimes moves to the bottom of the list of priorities, and if someone isn't taking personal responsibility for learning and practicing the faith, it'll be one of the first things to go. As you read this book, think about what steps of accountability you're taking to make sure you aren't tempted to hit the snooze button Sunday morning instead of going to Mass following your first late-Saturday-night social engagement. The Eucharist is true spiritual food, and the more connected you stay to this essential sacrament, the more strength you'll have to participate in it regularly and use the grace you receive from Jesus himself to grow in your faith amid the challenges of college life.

ALUMNI DIRECTORY
Saint Peter Gonzalez (1190–1246; Spain)

When it comes to saints who started off their lives taking their faith for granted, Saint Peter Gonzalez certainly makes the hall of shame. In thirteenth-century Spain, the royal family and many of the nobles were Catholic and had many clergy in high-profile positions in their courts. Saint Peter, who came from a prominent Catholic family, was interested in the priesthood, not so much because he had a deep sense of his vocation, but because he thought that by saying the right words and doing the right things, he could become a high-ranking clergy member with access to all the luxuries this particular office provided.

Saint Peter did, in fact, become ordained, and as he had hoped, gained increasing status in his early years as a priest. As his prominence increased, however, so did the size of his ego. The story goes that one Christmas, Saint Peter had planned a horseback procession through the streets of a local village. He was so vain that he had actually paid a large group of peasants to cheer him as he rode through town. Unfortunately for Peter, his plan backfired. When the people he'd paid to greet him erupted in praise, his horse became startled, and Peter was thrown from it into a large pile of livestock manure. As he rose from the rubbish and tried to clean himself up, Peter expected the peasants to be mortified at the offense to his dignity. Instead, he looked up to see them cackling with glee at the fact that some big shot had been taken down a notch.

That moment marked a point of conversion for Saint Peter. For the first time, he began to take ownership of his faith and of his priesthood, seeing it not merely as a status symbol or way to gain approval with certain people but as an opportunity to connect people with the sacraments. He repeatedly refused further offers to advance in the royal courts, choosing instead to move his ministry to the fringes of society, reaching out to the poor and marginalized, especially fisherman and dock workers. As such, he shows us that no matter how nominally Catholic you've been, there's always the opportunity to take your "official" faith and make it personal to change your life and impact others.

MEMORY VERSE

"But as for you, continue in what you have learned and firmly believed, knowing from whom you learned it, and how from childhood you have known the sacred writings that are able to instruct you for salvation through faith in Christ Jesus" (2 Timothy 3:14–15).

"Remember your creator in the days of your youth, before the days of trouble come, and the years draw near when you will say, 'I have no pleasure in them'" (Ecclesiastes 12:1).

CATECHISM OF THE CATHOLIC CHURCH
Faith

"Faith is a personal act—the free response of the human person to the initiative of God....But faith is not an isolated act. No one can believe alone, just as no one can live alone....The believer has received faith from others and should hand it on to others....Each believer is thus a link in the great chain of believers" (*CCC* 166).

Have you endeavored to hand on the faith to anyone? To whom and how so?

_____

_____

_____

_____

How comfortable are you with speaking to others about your faith?

_____

_____

_____

_____

How do you actively support other believers?

_____

_____

_____

_____

Extra Credit
Practical Steps Toward Owning Your College Faith

- Read great works of classic Catholic spirituality, such as some of the ones suggested at the end of this chapter. See if some of the Catholics you know on campus would be interested in participating in a discussion group based on these texts. If you don't have the time or patience for that, seek out an online message board where a conversation about matters of faith is taking place and join the discussion.

- In addition to finding an on-campus support system where you can sort out answers to your tough questions about the Church, consider signing up on an apologetics website like catholic.com or phatmass. com. Both of these sites have an open-source Q&A board where your questions can get responses from expert apologists as well as lay Catholics who are looking to settle the same issues you are.

- Find a patron saint whose life or writings you particularly connect with, and develop a relationship with this saint through prayer and study. Carry a medal or holy card of that saint with you, and have recourse to this heavenly intercessor as you face the everyday challenges to your faith.

SUGGESTED READING

In each chapter we provide a list of books you might want to pick up in the beginning stages of trying to take personal ownership of your faith related to the topic discussed in the chapter.

- *Theology for Beginners* by F. J. Sheed. A practical step-by-step guide through some of the most essential tenets of Catholicism. Sheed balances depth and clarity in a way that even a casual reader can appreciate. A must read for anyone who wants to get to the heart of what we believe as Catholics and why.

- *Mere Christianity* by C. S. Lewis. Lewis was not a Catholic, which he freely admits in the opening paragraphs of his book. However, his defense of why there is a God and why that God is the author of Christianity is unparalleled among Christian classical writers. This is one of those books that is worth reading once a year to remind yourself of the importance of being Christian.

- *Orthodoxy* by G. K. Chesterton. Chesterton wrote this book well over a decade before converting to Catholicism from the Church of England, but his mystical view of the world as viewed through the lens of Christianity has assisted a number of lukewarm Christians to get excited about their faith. His offbeat, witty, outside-the-box understanding of what it means to be Christian has opened the door for many Catholics to joyfully explore the depth of their faith.

PRAYER

Heavenly Father, thank you for inspiring my forebears in the faith to give me the gift of Christian creed, and especially for _____, who in particular has helped shape me as a believer. Aid me in taking the initiative to mature as a young-adult Catholic, seek eternal truth, and make you the center of my college experience. Give me the intellect, humility, and charity necessary to proclaim the Gospel, even when it is socially difficult. Put people in my life who can lead me deeper into love of you through worship, fellowship, service, and knowledge.

I ask this through Christ our Lord. Amen.

Finding Real Food on Campus: Getting Sacramentally Nourished

Jesus said to them, "Very truly, I tell you, unless you eat the flesh of the Son of Man and drink his blood, you have no life in you."

JOHN 6:53

Was it your parents who encouraged you to stay connected to the sacraments, or perhaps even your grandparents? Maybe you're one of the only members of your family who attends Mass regularly while your other siblings and even your parents stay home or devote Sundays to other activities. In any case, your relationship to Jesus in the Eucharist changes dramatically once you arrive at college.

In days past, your relationship with God and your relationship with your parents may have felt somewhat interchangeable. You received from your parents whatever understanding you have of right and wrong (in some cases, by witnessing their mistakes), and you learned how to interact with authority (in some cases, by making your own mistakes). Now that you've left the nest, it's time to take your understanding of right, wrong, and the way you deal with life's largest questions to a new level.

What role have the sacraments played in your life? Are you someone who was baptized at birth and has been to Mass every Sunday since—or maybe most Sundays, depending on your sports schedule? How often do you keep holy the Sabbath, as required by the Fourth Commandment?

_____

_____

_____

_____

Why It's Important to Take This Chapter Seriously

Most college students begin their new educational situation living on campus, most likely in a dorm or other campus housing. That means prioritizing the sacraments will be harder for you in the days ahead than ever. Not only do you no longer necessarily have another adult who lives in the same building and who is getting you up for Mass on Sundays, but you have to deal with factors that work against whatever instincts you have toward prioritizing the Eucharist. Sunday mornings on college campuses typically follow late-Saturday-night social engagements, and hitting the snooze button after staying up until 3:00 AM suddenly becomes more appealing. If regular Mass has been a part of your spiritual life, it will become far more difficult to incorporate as you stay up late studying for the latest and most pressing exam. And it's unlikely that any RA, professor, or roommate will be constantly reminding you how important it is to keep the sacraments a part of your life.

During high school, what factors were temptations against the commandment to keep the Sabbath holy?

_____

_____

_____

_____

So how common is it for college students to quickly become C&E (Christmas and Easter) or CME (Christmas, Mother's Day, and Easter) Catholics? The statistics are pretty sobering, and in a college setting, sober is usually a good thing. Georgetown University's Center for Applied Research in the Apostolate (CARA) indicates that those first weeks of college are when you're most likely to meet the best friends you'll have for the next four years, give or take, and it's also the time when you're most likely to join whatever campus organizations you'll be a part of for the duration of your college career ("Bridging the College Faith Gap," *National Catholic Register,* December 3, 2010). People familiar with college students know how vulnerable you are at this transitional period of your life. And if you're not careful, all of these new opportunities and responsibilities will tear you away from your Catholic identity before you even realize what's happened. Additionally, even on Catholic campuses, CARA surveys indicate that only 57 percent of students remain practicing Catholics at some level or other from orientation to graduation. So what is it that's tearing collegiate Catholics away from the sacraments that helped shape their identity, often from infancy through their senior year of high school? Many factors are responsible: such as the appeal of a sexually immoral campus life, parties where it seems anything and everything is permissible, professors who seem to delight in confusing the moral compasses of students, and the biggest factor of all—apathy in general, wherein you don't go to Mass or confession because you just don't feel like it.

But why should you feel like receiving the sacraments? The *Catechism of the Catholic Church* reminds us: "The mission of the Holy Spirit in the liturgy of the Church is to prepare the assembly to encounter Christ; to recall and manifest Christ to the faith of the assembly; to make the saving work of Christ present and active by his transforming power; and to make the gift of communion bear fruit in the Church" (1112).

So what does this mean? It means that Jesus intends for us to encounter him in a number of ways: in an extraordinary sunset, in relationships with friends and family, in the face of the poor, and in other ways that we find listed throughout the Scriptures. But there is one way that he calls us to encounter him that transcends all others, and that is through the Eucharist. The liturgy, as the *Catechism* states, prepares us to encounter Christ, manifests him uniquely before us, facilitates his transforming power in our lives, and gives us the grace to bear the fruit of a life lived in Christ. It is about this encounter that he tells us so very clearly, "Unless you eat the flesh of the Son of Man and drink his blood, you do not have life within you" (John 6:53, NAB). Why would you want to face all of the challenging temptations, life decisions, and emotional ups and downs that go along with the college experience without equipping yourself with sacramental armor?

There is, however, an essential and far more neglected sacrament that should be a part of every Catholic college student's life if they want to remain connected to the life of Christ, and that is the sacrament of reconciliation, or as it's commonly called, confession. This is not a popular sacrament; in fact, it may be the least popular of all sacraments. Who wants to air their dirty laundry in front of another person, especially a person whose life is supposed to be devoted to the work of God? How intimidating is it to talk about your own lack of holiness to someone whose job it is to be holy?

When was the last time you went to confession? What parishes in close proximity to campus housing offer this sacrament during a time that is most feasible given your schedule? Are you willing to put regular confession on your calendar like you would a class?

_____

_____

_____

_____

_____

Many college students stop going to confession, if they were even going in the first place, because the most commonly offered time for confession is Saturday afternoon. It's possible that many have a subconscious fear that whatever they might engage in a few hours later might negate whatever would be accomplished in the confessional, given the temptations so freely available on college campuses. This is not a good reason to avoid this sacrament.

Have you ever avoided the sacrament of reconciliation in the past? If so, what was your excuse?

_____

_____

_____

_____

_____

Nearly every campus ministry or parish provides an opportunity to receive the sacrament of reconciliation on-demand by simply making an appointment with the pastor. Very few pastors, unless they have pressing responsibilities, will refuse even an on-the-spot confession request. You may even find it helpful to locate a parish within walking distance (especially if you don't have a car) and put their sacramental schedule on your mini-fridge or tack it to a corkboard in your dorm room—wherever you know you'll see it. That way, every time you reach for a snack or check your class schedule, you'll at least be reminded of the gift God is offering to you in your own neighborhood. You'll also be reminded how part of this maturing process that you experience during your college years involves your taking the responsibility to own up to your sins and to stay in communion with Christ.

After all, avoiding the sacraments is classified among the sins against justice. Justice means that deserving persons should get what they deserve. And if God deserves our repentance and our reception of him in the Eucharist, we're being unjust if we ignore God's call to connect with him in those ways. Without a doubt, a lot of forces in your college experience will try to compel you to act on issues of justice. However, unless your sense of justice is rooted in confession and the Eucharist, you will have a harder time than necessary discerning the difference between justice and simply being nice to people, because sometimes giving people what they want isn't necessarily just. In the same way, it's important to come to the understanding that God is not just some benevolent overlord who wants you to always feel good about yourself. If sin and redemption exist, which as Catholics we profess they do, it's important to stay connected to the sacraments, even in an environment such as a college campus where participation in them can easily be dismissed.

When does your Catholic campus ministry or the nearest parish to your college offer confession?

_____

_____

_____

_____

Of course, two other sacraments will likely come into play in a major way during your college years, namely, the sacrament of marriage and the sacrament of holy orders. We'll discuss both in greater detail in a later chapter, but the majority of you who are reading this will be entering into marriage, and through your own experience, you know that many of the married couples you grew up with met in college. That means the chances are good that you could meet your own spouse during your higher-educational experience.

This should help you want to make the sacramental life even more of a priority during your college years. Most people want to marry someone who makes them a better person. If you prioritize the sacraments, that will very likely put you in contact with others who also prioritize them. This, then, makes it more likely that your spouse will share your values and that you'll grow together along a mutual path toward holiness. Many people who enter a marriage with mixed spiritual priorities end up having to deal with complicated religious tensions later on, especially once children arrive.

What religious faith do your parents practice? What impact did this have on your upbringing?

_____

_____

_____

_____

Additionally, it's quite common for inconsistently practicing Catholics, and even some non-Catholics, to approach beautiful churches they have not regularly attended and ask them to host their wedding. Though it is likely that the Church will welcome you to enter into a covenant relationship through the sacrament of marriage, your participation in the overall life of the Church—the body of Christ—is essential. Marriage isn't intended as a spectacle but as a life-giving sacrament that gives witness to the world of the love of Christ for the people of God. Unfortunately, it is easy for someone who isn't involved in the sacramental life to miss that.

You may be surprised to know that if you go to a Catholic college or university, you might encounter professors, some of them even priests, deacons, or religious, who believe and even teach something totally different than what the Church teaches about the sacraments. In recent years, at least two such Catholic theologians have had books censured—not censored—by the Vatican. Not censored, of course, means that the Church has made no effort to stop their publication, just an effort to clarify why these writings can't be considered consistent with Catholic teaching. Does this mean the theology professors who have written these works are bad people? Not necessarily. All it means is that in their search for the truth, their speculations have led them down paths that are probably more accurately defined as modernist and secular than Catholic.

It can be easy to take one of two approaches to such professors, especially when it comes to sacramental theology. One can either demonize them entirely and see them as persons bent on undermining the mission of the Church or (and this is very common in academic pursuits) become so open-minded that your brain eventually falls out of your head. In other words, don't totally dismiss a professor just because you disagree with him or her, but don't automatically dismiss the questions posed, because they can provide opportunities for further understanding in regard to the sacramental life.

Your college years offer you a unique opportunity to make your faith your own rather than just something you inherited. Use challenging questions to explore your beliefs, and put those beliefs to the test by recognizing the truth of what the Church teaches in an intensely personal way. Bear in mind that you may run into the occasional professor who actually takes satisfaction in undermining the worldviews of his or her students. Don't let this dishearten you or cause you to react to him or her in the way he or she hopes you will. Of course, the majority of your professors won't be like that. Just be prepared for the possibility that you'll meet one who will.

Be Intentional

Most campus environments are saturated with things to keep students busy: organizations, parties, athletics, concerts, and probably most important, studying. In any case, all of these activities, though not necessarily bad in and of themselves, stand a serious chance of crowding the sacraments out of your schedule. If you don't make it a point to participate in the sacraments, they might be the first thing to drop from your agenda.

What are the top three student groups, organizations, teams, or activities you would like to prioritize during your college experience?

_____

_____

_____

There's a decent chance you have a smartphone, but even if you have a dumbphone, you probably have scheduling software on your tablet, laptop, or desktop computer. You can set reminders before you even go to orientation to ping you on certain days and at certain times to let you know that whatever else is going on, it's time to go to Mass or, depending on how your week on campus has gone, confession (you'll know when it's time). Or if you're the kind of person who prefers to keep a hard-copy, write it on your calendar in permanent marker. Whatever method works in your particular situation, put reminders where you know you'll actually be reminded. Otherwise, some engagement or other will either conflict with your sacramental participation or, more likely, you'll realize it's time to go to church just a bit too late. Then rather than rushing off to your parish, you'll just abandon your responsibility altogether and convince yourself you'll go next time. It's all too easy in a college environment to completely rationalize yourself out of being a practicing Catholic. However, with a little effort, you can maintain your home routine (or start going back to church if you didn't go with your family).

Look up Mass times on your campus, as many parishes and Newman Centers provide Sunday-evening Masses for your convenience. However, there's a chance that sacraments in close proximity to your campus might not be all that readily available. Perhaps the campus chapel only offers one Mass per week, and confession only by appointment. Don't use these excuses to divorce yourself from the sacramental life. Perhaps the reason they're only offering reconciliation and Mass as infrequently as they are is due to lack of demand. What if your regular participation encouraged them to offer the sacraments with more regularity and more of your fellow students who were on the fence in regard to going to church were more inclined to do so as a result? You never know how your witness of receiving the Eucharist might influence others, even those you do not know.

What are the Mass times of your campus ministry or local parish?

_____

_____

_____

_____

When is Eucharistic Adoration offered on or near your campus?

_____

_____

_____

_____

You will likely be presented with a gazillion different worldviews that aren't exactly what one might call Catholic in your experience as a college student. This chapter is not designed to help you respond to atheists, although you will encounter many of them in college, who take unbelief as an article of faith and believe absolutely that there is no such thing as absolute truth. Deal with them in charity and, to paraphrase the hymn, *Let Them Know You Are Christians by Your Love.* Some guidelines for dialogue with atheists will be discussed in the chapter on social media.

Another group of well-meaning people, though, will very likely seem appealing to you, especially if you're inclined toward belief in Jesus and a charitable outlook on interactions with those who don't subscribe to the Catholic faith. Non-Catholic Christians are well known for their love of Christ, for which they ought to be commended. However, as a Catholic, you should be aware of some messages they may present. One of them is the idea that your relationship with God should be so personal that there is no need for any authoritative body such as the Catholic Church's hierarchical structure. In other words, your relationship with God should be your business and nobody else's—not that of your parents, your friends, not even the Church.

On the surface, this sounds great and pure. Why dilute a connection between you and the Creator of the universe by inserting some committee or organization into the discussion? The reason for remaining connected to the Church, which has many committees and organizations, is simpler than it might seem. For your Christian friends who don't accept Catholicism but who are seeking the well-being of your soul, an elementary question might help: "Who has the authority to interpret Scripture?" Chances are, if you were to attend an event hosted by a generally Christian campus ministry, you'd get a common answer: The Holy Spirit, who speaks to the heart of the individual believer, has the authority to interpret the Bible.

This sounds like an empowering and appealing thought until you begin to understand that this line of thinking has led to the fracturing of Christian unity for centuries. In a conversation between two Christians who disagree on the interpretation of Scripture, who's to say the Holy Spirit isn't speaking to both of them? Things can get pretty relativistic quite quickly if you're not careful with this kind of self-centered approach to Christianity. Just like non-Catholic Christians, our faith should be rooted in a personal relationship with Jesus Christ. But when we understand how Christ mediates himself to us through the life of the Church, and in particular through the sacraments, we can live our faith joyfully and be powerful witnesses to those who might see Catholicism as just a bunch of rules.

> The truth is, of course, that the curtness of the Ten Commandments is an evidence, not of the gloom and narrowness of a religion, but, on the contrary, of its liberality and humanity. It is shorter to state the things forbidden than the things permitted: precisely because most things are permitted, and only a few things are forbidden.—G. K. Chesterton

As mentioned earlier, one of the things that will help you stay rooted in your Catholic faith during your college years is seeking out friends who share your values. One good way to do this is by connecting with Catholic campus ministries that may have a presence at your school, such as a Newman Center or through FOCUS or Catholic-faith outreach groups. These ministries naturally attract people who are looking to maintain the practice of their faith and who are looking for others who are trying to do the same. The nondenominational Christian campus outreach may or may not have better music, better pizza, or even more creative ways of engaging you, but do they have the Eucharist? Nondenominational campus ministries can be great places to meet Christian friends and enjoy college life in a wholesome environment, but if your participation in them is pulling you away from the sacraments, they're not the place for you. Plugging into a Catholic campus ministry and meeting other Catholic students will help to keep at the forefront of your mind why the sacraments are vital to the Christian life. Protestant campus ministers are usually wonderful people, and you can find some great common ground with them in terms of your mutual love for Christ. Just don't forget which Church Jesus founded in the process.

ALUMNI DIRECTORY
Saint Tarcisius (third century; Rome)

How serious did Saint Tarcisius take the sacramental life? As it turns out, he was transporting a consecrated Host, for whatever reason, when he was attacked by a pagan mob who, in a time when society was extremely hostile to Christianity, wanted to make an example of him.

Sources differ, but it's said that as he was being beaten to death, those who sought to desecrate the Eucharist couldn't find any consecrated Hosts once Tarcisius had been murdered. Some accounts record that this is because he had rapidly consumed the Eucharist before his attackers were able to desecrate it. In any case, Saint Tarcisius is a shining example of the kind of courage one can exhibit when faced with the meaning of the sacraments in a life-or-death situation.

Today, the Church considers Saint Tarcisius the patron saint of altar servers and first Communicants, since his dedication to the preservation of the Blessed Sacrament was so great that he was willing to give up his life rather than see our Lord subjected to blasphemy and desecration. His witness should stand as an example to all of us who want to take more seriously our devotion to the sacraments.

MEMORY VERSE

"Abide in me as I abide in you. Just as the branch cannot bear fruit by itself unless it abides in the vine, neither can you unless you abide in me" (John 15:4).

CATECHISM OF THE CATHOLIC CHURCH
Participation in Sunday Eucharist

Missing Sunday Mass is a slippery slope, and missing once without grave reason makes it easier to come up with excuses to sleep in or just plain skip out again in the future, thus quickly making it a habit. Taking it seriously will help to cement your Sunday priorities and witness to what is important, hopefully the source and summit of your faith life.

"The Sunday Eucharist is the foundation and confirmation of all Christian practice. For this reason the faithful are obliged to participate in the Eucharist on days of obligation, unless excused for a serious reason (for example, illness, the care of infants) or dispensed by their own pastor. Those who deliberately fail in this obligation commit a grave sin" (*CCC* 2181).

EXTRA CREDIT
Practical Steps Toward Living More Sacramentally

- If you're looking for an easy way to invite your friends to Mass or share your faith on campus, try going to Mass on Ash Wednesday. It's a very interactive liturgy, and getting ashes on the first day of Lent can be a great conversation starter with fellow students.

- Figure out early on which friends will encourage you to go to Mass and which friends will encourage you to do almost anything in the world but go to Mass. Try to plan Saturday activities with your Mass-going friends—maybe Saturday-afternoon confession, Mass, pizza, and then a movie or video-game night. You could be one of the only people on your hall who doesn't wake up in the middle of the day on Sunday regretting what you did the night before.

- If at all possible, incorporate at least one daily Mass into your week. Put it into your schedule like you would a biology class. Making this work is easier than you might realize; daily Mass is usually less than a half-hour long, and prioritizing it can make a huge difference in the way you approach your week.

- Not all campuses offer this opportunity, but if you know of a place nearby that offers Eucharistic Adoration, make a note of it. We've all been at that point where we're so distracted and burned out that we can't concentrate on anything. When you hit that point, visit an Adoration chapel, even if only for ten minutes.

- Put confession on your calendar. If you know you need confession immediately, then by all means take care of it on the spot. Aside from that, though, regular participation in the sacrament of reconciliation can have an extraordinarily renewing effect on the soul. Look at your school calendar and think of the times when you'll most need God's mercy during a semester or trimester. Maybe you can schedule a trip to the confessional to coincide with finals' week or the conclusion of a major paper or project. The perspective you'll gain may just spill over positively into your classwork.

SUGGESTED READING

- *Sacraments in Scripture: Salvation History Made Present* by Tim Gray; foreword by Scott Hahn. These two college professors take a look at the way the Bible sets the stage for the sacraments we appreciate today, beginning with their roots in the Hebrew Scriptures. This book is a great way to understand the scriptural basis for a Catholic understanding of the means God has ordained for our salvation.

- *The Lamb's Supper: The Mass as Heaven on Earth* by Scott Hahn. Dr. Hahn does an excellent job of explaining the mysterious Book of Revelation in the context of the Mass—a great way to connect the most apocalyptic book in the Bible with the regular experience of holy Communion.

- *The Sacraments We Celebrate: A Catholic Guide to the Seven Mysteries of Faith* by Peter J. Vaghi. Msgr. Vaghi breaks down the essential components of each sacrament and why they're necessary and explains why the Catholic Church prioritizes the sacraments in the way it does. An excellent resource for anyone having difficulty understanding why ritual is important.

PRAYER

Down in adoration falling
This great Sacrament we hail
Over ancient forms of worship
Newer rites of grace prevail
Faith will tell us Christ is present
When our human senses fail.

To the everlasting Father
And the Son who made us free
And the Spirit God proceeding
From them each eternally
Be salvation, honor, blessing
Might and endless majesty. Amen.

SAINT THOMAS AQUINAS

Making It Morally: Living Christian Ethics in the Dorms

Living in this changing culture with a desire for truth and an attitude of service in conformity with the Christian ideal, has, at times, become difficult. In the past, becoming a student, and even more so a professor, was everywhere an unquestionable social promotion. Today, the context of university studies is often marked by new difficulties, of a material or moral order, that rapidly become human and spiritual problems with unforeseeable consequences.

THE PRESENCE OF THE CHURCH IN THE UNIVERSITY
AND IN UNIVERSITY CULTURE, 3

Whether you're an only child or come from a large family, you've had to live in some kind of communal situation at least a few times throughout your life. That means living with people you might not always get along with, sharing responsibilities, accommodating the needs of others, and occasionally sacrificing your own interests for the sake of the greater good of the people you're living with. You've probably roomed with someone at a retreat or camp and felt completely different about that person after a few days in close proximity. Living on campus can be likened to those experiences, only with more community members, less supervision, and more responsibility.

What is your most memorable pre-college communal living situation outside of your immediate family? How/why did it have an impact on you?

_____

_____

_____

_____

_____

_____

_____

_____

The choice to live on campus might take you ten miles away or ten states away from your family, but in either case, dorm life is going to be unlike any living situation you've ever experienced. You'll face new kinds of annoyances, forge different sorts of bonds, endure unfamiliar and untried degrees of temptation, and engage in increasing levels of responsibility. Being grounded in your faith is extremely important when it comes to living on a college campus for all of these reasons and more.

What are the top three qualities you would want in an ideal roommate?

_____

_____

_____

_____

_____

Why It's Important to Take This Chapter Seriously

Unless you're the luckiest person who has ever attended college in the history of higher education, you are going to run into some conflict with your roommates or housemates. This can take many forms: maybe you're a late sleeper when your roommate is an early riser, perhaps you differ on standards of cleanliness, or it could be that your tastes in music and movies are so different that you wonder what planet your roommate came from. Your roommates might do certain things that annoy you to no end, as you may have experienced with siblings, cousins, or close friends; but remember, these may be subconscious actions on their part. It can be easy to become bitter and angry, and feel like you do not have a home even in your own dorm.

However, just because you may no longer be living with the personality conflicts that might have been present in your home doesn't mean you've graduated from the experience of living with annoyances. Even if you marry the perfect person, you're still going to have to engage in conflict resolution from time to time—probably on a daily basis. Campus life gives you an opportunity to learn compromise on a whole new level to create a more harmonious living situation. This does not mean compromising your Catholic values or identity, but instead some of your preferences that may not even be that important in the big picture, though it could be uncomfortable in the moment.

If you find yourself being consumed by frustration over things your roommate does, take a step back and make your own examination of conscience. Is there something in your personality or perhaps in the way you operate that might be a source of annoyance to others? As Jesus tells us in Matthew 7:3, "Why do you see the speck in your neighbor's eye, but do not notice the log in your own eye?"

It's highly important to avoid two extremes in dealing with roommate conflict. Don't nitpick every single thing your roommate does that gets on your nerves (this can especially manifest itself in the passive-aggressive stickie note, dry-erase board memo, or text message). Also, however, don't hold in everything until you finally explode at the person who gets on your nerves. Handling these kinds of situations with right judgment means compromise and finding the *via media*, the middle way.

What is a quirk of your own that others might find challenging to live with?

_____

_____

_____

_____

_____

In high school, you probably faced the classic temptations all adolescents face in one form or another, what Baptist preachers in the 1950s referred to as the "evils of sex, drugs, and rock n' roll." Your parents or guardians may or may not have had you on a short leash during high school, and presently they may still try to keep you close to the nest even though you're either getting ready to go to college or have been there a while. Regardless, you're entering a situation in which you have to bear more responsibility than you've ever had when it comes to avoiding temptation—and that situation is one in which temptation shows up on your doorstep without your even taking the trouble to seek it out.

This will require an increasing amount of self-control, which will be necessary in all kinds of situations, from living morally on campus to seeking wisdom both in and out of the undergraduate classroom. As the lives of the saints can repeatedly tell us through their own struggles toward holiness, there's no compartmentalizing when it comes to striving to become saints. Shortcomings, especially lack of discipline, in one aspect of our lives can have dire consequences for other aspects of our lives. If we can't create boundaries for ourselves when it comes to the little things in life, how can we possibly expect to master problems of great consequence? True freedom is found by exercising self-control, and it is only when embracing this principle that you will be able to do what you truly want, both in college as well as in the greater post-graduate world. Freedom is not the ability to do whatever you want; rather, freedom is the possibility of doing what you ought to do. And doing what you ought to do is in reality what you most deeply desire, for right judgment brings order and justice to the world as well as within your own life.

What approach did your parent(s) or guardian(s) take in terms of discipline during your high school years? Do you feel like it was an appropriate philosophy? Why or why not?

_____

_____

_____

_____

_____

Campus culture can often be an extremely sexualized environment, even at many Catholic colleges. High schoolers who hit puberty half a decade ago are now out from under their parents' supervision, and those who may or may not have had opportunities for sexual experimentation will suddenly have them in superabundance. Colleges, even some that come from a Catholic tradition, can often take a lazy approach to campus life on issues of sexual morality, assuming that college students are going to be sexually active no matter what. So colleges simply provide students with resources to avoid pregnancy and sexually transmitted diseases. Many secular colleges (as well as some Catholic ones) have coed dormitories and offer only mildly restricted visitation policies. That means sexual temptations will literally be on your doorstep on a regular basis.

It's up to you to create boundaries for yourself to ensure your own dorm room is not an occasion for sexual sin, and the earlier you do so, the better. This can be achieved in part by being intentional about where you decide to live on campus. You might begin by selecting a single-sex dorm. Additionally, you may want to contact the local Catholic campus ministry to see if they have any tips on what living situations might have a better moral reputation than others. Chances are, they'll know, as word tends to get out about these kinds of things.

As for your own personal responsibility, you'll need to be continually reminding yourself of who you are as a child of God and how you should be treating others by remembering that they, too, are God's children. We hope you've been privileged to have what the Declaration on Christian Education refers to as a "positive and prudent sexual education," including parental role models who have demonstrated human sexuality in its most loving and life-giving context through their committed marital relationship. Many of you may not have had the best mentors in this respect, but that doesn't let you off the hook. Check out some of the great resources on Christian chastity and the theology of the body at the end of this chapter, and seek out the guidance of married couples, such as parents, grandparents, uncles and aunts, neighbors, godparents, or teachers who have been models of marital fidelity. Though their relationships may not necessarily have been perfect, many of them are striving for holiness. In the end, you are not destined to make the same mistakes of those who have gone before you, but you might need a bit of extra help to avoid some of the pitfalls.

Know your limits when it comes to chastity. Avoid an occasion of sin, that is, a situation you might not be strong enough to handle. This can include circumstances like spending extended time alone in a private location with someone you are or could be sexually attracted to, especially by allowing that person to spend the night or stay over extremely late; willingly allowing yourself to do drugs or drink excessively to lose your inhibitions; or hanging with people simply to hook up. God invites us to respect the dignity of others and to enter into friendship with them. We are not intended to merely use others for temporary pleasure, but to recognize the gift God has given each of us as embodied people. Pay close attention when your conscience is telling you to slow down and hold back. When temptations come along, it may be helpful to invoke the prayers of powerful intercessors of chastity, such as Saint Joseph, Saint Maria Goretti, and Saint Thomas Aquinas, who is the patron saint of both chaste living and college students!

Another major temptation college students face involves substance abuse. Underage drinking is almost a staple of campus life these days, and it's rarely effectively policed by campus security or resident assistants. You may be shocked at how readily available alcohol and even drugs are in your own dormitory. For some upperclassmen, it's almost a badge of honor to get a younger student wasted who's never been drunk before or to get someone to smoke pot for the first time. There's nothing wrong with drinking alcohol moderately as a college student who's legally old enough to do so, but moderation isn't usually encouraged in dormitory culture.

Just remember, you don't have to party your brains (or in some cases, your guts) out to have a fulfilling college experience. If you do exercise your free will to that extent, there's a good chance you'll end up being bereft of a scholarship, getting your stomach pumped, taken advantage of, or in some other equally unenviable position. These outcomes are not fulfilling and will likely contribute to unwelcome stress as you try to advance toward adulthood. And when you become an upperclassman, don't take pride in "breaking in" some sheltered freshman. There's a high probability that not every person in your incoming class will live to see graduation, and alcohol-related incidents remain the number-one cause of death among college students. Furthermore, your body is a temple of the Holy Spirit, and abusing it is disrespectful to the One who gave it to you.

Did you face temptations to abuse drugs and alcohol during your high school years? If so, how did you respond to them? How do you plan to respond to them in college?

_____

_____

_____

_____

_____

_____

_____

_____

_____

While we're talking about dormitory temptations, it's important to note the prevalence of pornography and other negative forms of media that are often readily available in college dorms. Your campus Internet provider may block some pornographic material from making it into your computer or that of your dorm mates, but it's impossible to block everything. In addition, you'll be exposed to music, movies, and an entire culture that likely won't share your Catholic values and may even be hostile to them, so it's important to be aware of your media choices. Getting together with a group of people in a dorm room to watch a movie may seem harmless on the surface (and most of the time it is), but bear in mind that what goes into your head in that setting is likely to stay there a lot longer than most of what you learn in freshman biology class. There's a good chance that nobody will be looking over your shoulder to tell you that what you're listening to or watching in your dorm is good or bad for you; you have to practice discernment and self-control now more than ever.

In his Apostolic Constitution on Catholic Universities, *Ex Corde Ecclesiae* ("From the Heart of the Church"), John Paul II states, "If need be, a Catholic University must have the courage to speak uncomfortable truths which do not please public opinion, but which are necessary to safeguard the authentic good of society" (32). If you're attending a Catholic university, this mission is hopefully carried out as a whole by the institution, from the administration to the professors to the student groups. But no matter where you are, this calling to be morally courageous is also extended to the individual college or university student, for whom every day may entail facing uncomfortable truths. As crazy or as scary as it may seem, it's really quite simple. As a result you could come out of college a little worse for the wear, or tried and true, a better person than you were when you lived at home. After investing an incredible amount of time, emotional energy, and financial resources, the obvious choice is to make sure that, while the experiences you have are not totally up to you, you are called to react to them in a way that does you proud and makes the college years ones to look back on without avoidable moral regrets.

ALUMNI DIRECTORY
Saint Monica (331–387; born in modern-day Algeria and died in Rome) and Saint Augustine (354–430; born and died in modern-day Algeria)

Saint Monica was an alcoholic. She had a habit of sneaking wine while fetching it for her superiors, a fact we know because Saint Augustine, her son, recorded it in his *Confessions*. Saint Augustine didn't have the best moral track record either; he conceived a child out of wedlock while exploring pagan philosophies.

Somehow, both of these sinners are considered saints by the Church. Saint Monica, who snuck booze while bringing drinks to her superiors, and Saint Augustine, who was admittedly promiscuous, had conversions; both realized they were going down the wrong path and corrections had to be made. Saint Augustine went on to become one of the greatest thinkers in the Western world, primarily because he understood the value of the Christian life in the midst of worldly temptations. Augustine was not chaste prior to his conversion, but he took his experiences and used them as a way to promote a true Catholic perspective on sexuality.

Both Monica and Augustine faced challenges to living the authentic Christian life, but both exhibited humility and a sense of surrender as they tried to submit their own temptations to Catholic teachings as to what it means to be moral. In the Roman Empire in the fourth century, Saint Augustine's countercultural views would live on to instruct many thinkers who lived long after the fall of Rome.

MEMORY VERSE

"Do not be conformed to this world, but be transformed by the renewing of your minds, so that you may discern what is the will of God—what is good and acceptable and perfect" (Romans 12:2).

Are you conformed to this age, setting as your standard what others and our media-saturated age say is moral, or do you base your ideas of what is virtuous and righteous on the principles set out by God in his sacred Scriptures and Tradition? Give two examples.

_____

_____

_____

_____

_____

_____

_____

_____

_____

_____

CATECHISM OF THE CATHOLIC CHURCH
The Battle for Purity

"Purity of heart brings freedom from widespread eroticism and avoids entertainment inclined to voyeurism and illusion" (*CCC* 2525).

"So-called *moral permissiveness* rests on an erroneous conception of human freedom; the necessary precondition for the development of true freedom is to let oneself be educated in the moral law" (*CCC* 2526).

"The Good News of Christ continually renews the life and culture of fallen man; it combats and removes the error and evil which flow from the ever-present attraction of sin" (*CCC* 2527).

EXTRA CREDIT
Practical Steps Toward Living Christian Ethics

- Post your favorite prayer where you know only you can find it (perhaps even as a note on your smartphone), and pray it whenever you become particularly annoyed with a roommate.

- If you plan to participate in dorm, sorority, or fraternity activities where you know sex, drugs, or underage and imprudent use of alcohol will be involved, avoid them. These are occasions that could steer you in the wrong direction and thus tempt you to do things you might regret. If you unwittingly participate in a dorm, sorority, or fraternity activity where these vices are most definitely involved, plan your escape. Perhaps you have outstanding homework responsibilities, somewhere to be the next morning, or something else you know you should be doing once you see a party getting out of control. Don't be ashamed to invoke these as reasons to leave, even if you have to invoke them multiple times before someone actually lets you off the hook. Or get a friend to call and invite you elsewhere. If you have the courage, speak up and tell your friends that you do not like the turn the gathering has made. Your fortitude could even assist others at these gatherings to make wise choices about how they want to spend their time. One never knows how she or he will touch or make a difference in another's life.

- Saint Isidore of Seville is the patron saint of the Internet. Try posting a prayer for his intercession somewhere near your computer workstation before logging on so that when temptations to engage in unhealthy Internet activity arise, it will be handy. The prayer can be found at the end of Chapter Eight.

- Make it a point to learn not only the names of the people you live with, but also the names of their parents and siblings. You would be surprised at how this simple gesture will help you understand their life situations all the more. In so doing, they might become more open to reaching out to you if and when they run into difficult situations. Although you most certainly will not have all the answers for them, taking an interest in your housing partners beyond the mere fact that they exist on campus is a practical step to recognizing their dignity as someone made in God's image and likeness. And likely, regardless of how difficult or obstinate another may seem, it is quite likely they have a lesson to teach you about yourself as well as God. Some of our greatest lessons are taught through people, especially those who challenge us to see things differently.

SUGGESTED READING

- *The Thrill of the Chaste* by Dawn Eden. Eden is a convert from Judaism to Catholicism and a former headline writer for the *New York Post* and a reporter for *Rolling Stone*. Her experience of the overly sexualized culture the mainstream media can encourage led her to realize the beauty of the Church's teaching on sexuality. She's frank, honest, and extremely down to earth in addressing the issues faced by today's Catholics who live in an oversexualized age.

- *Confessions* by Saint Augustine. If anyone knew the struggle between living the Catholic life and succumbing to the temptations of this world, it was Saint Augustine. While he was pursuing academic interests as a brilliant intellectual, he also managed to father a child out of wedlock and was an all-around hedonist before being smacked in the forehead with the truth of the Catholic faith. His personal account of how this all came about is considered not only one of the greatest Catholic works of all time but also one of the greatest Western literary works. It is widely studied in universities all over the world.

- *How to Find Your Soulmate Without Losing Your Soul* by Jason and Crystalina Evert. The Everts do a great job of showing the true meaning of Catholic sexuality. Jason once struggled with a porn addiction, and Crystalina struggled with all the sexual difficulties that accompany a woman's teenage and young-adult years. Their experience has helped a number of struggling Catholics, as has their book.

- *Set Free to Love: Lives Changed by the Theology of the Body* by Marcel LeJeune. In this book, LeJeune, a campus minister at Texas A&M University, has put together stories of people who, after fighting past cultural misconceptions as to what the Church has to say about sex, found themselves blown away by the depth and beauty of Church teaching in this area. This is a collection of down-to-earth personal testimonies from people who went through a discovery process that led them to an experience of love and beauty that can only come from a Christ-centered understanding of the meaning of sex and the body.

PRAYER

Saint Augustine, you are living proof that the greatest of sinners can be even greater saints. Intercede for me to obtain the courage to live a life of Christian morality, exercising the grace of self-control to pursue the demands of academic life and purity of body and soul.

Help me especially to be kind in my interactions with roommates, wise in my attitude toward alcohol and drugs, and on guard against obscene imagery. Amen.

AVERSION
by John A. Hardon, SJ

Lord Jesus, help me to overcome the aversion I feel for this person. Enlighten me to see your presence in him, so that captivated by this image I may not be distracted by his natural temperament or deceived by external appearances.

Teach me to observe in him only his virtues and good qualities, and in myself only my faults and imperfections. You have placed him into my life as an opportunity to prove my love for you and as a way to expiate, in some measure, the impatience that my own failings and defects have provoked in others. Amen.

Catholic Community
on Campus and Beyond

The presence of young university students trained and anxious to communicate to their peers the fruitfulness of the Christian faith, not only in Europe but throughout the world, is very important.

POPE BENEDICT, DECEMBER 16, 2010,
CELEBRATION OF VESPERS WITH UNIVERSITY STUDENTS AND
TEACHERS OF ROME IN PREPARATION FOR CHRISTMAS

Although it's important that our Catholic faith be centered in a personal relationship with Christ, it's also significant to note that Jesus doesn't want us to make our journey toward unity with him by ourselves. He founded the Church because he knew the importance of Christian community in the spiritual development of individual believers.

The approach you take to Catholic community as a college student will lay the foundation for the way you connect with fellow Catholics in your parish and beyond once you graduate. So it's crucial to recognize now what gifts you bring to the community and what you're capable of taking on in your interactions with other believers. This will not only assist you to share these gifts with those in college, but also to contribute to other communities you choose to join after college.

Why It's Important to Take This Chapter Seriously

In his First Letter to the Corinthians, Saint Paul likens the Church to a human body, the individual parts of which have specific and necessary functions but cannot perform those functions unless they're attached to the rest of the body. He makes very clear the significance of Christian community in his analogy:

"For just as the body is one and has many members, and all the members of the body, though many, are one body, so it is with Christ. For in the one Spirit we were all baptized into one body—Jews or Greeks, slaves or free—and we were all made to drink of one Spirit.

"Indeed, the body does not consist of one member but of many. If the foot were to say, 'Because I am not a hand, I do not belong to the body,' that would not make it any less a part of the body. And if the ear were to say, 'Because I am not an eye, I do not belong to the body,' that would not make it any less a part of the body. If the whole body were an eye, where would the hearing be? If the whole body were hearing, where would the sense of smell be? But as it is, God arranged the members in the body, each one of them, as he chose. If all were a single member, where would the body be? As it is, there are many members, yet one body"(12:12–20).

Later, he ties the symbolism together: "Now you are the body of Christ and individually members of it" (1 Corinthians 12:27). You may be a hand, foot, ear, or eye in the body of Christ, but just as surely as the body needs you, you need the body. As you spend your time developing your skills and knowledge for a career path, don't forget that this is also an optimal time to develop the virtues and gifts that can benefit not only yourself but the wider Catholic community.

Parish communities can be an amalgam of all types of people from many different careers, families, and socioeconomic backgrounds; but spiritual gifts often transcend the social categories we tend to build up in our minds and hearts. The gifts of wisdom, understanding, counsel, fortitude, knowledge, piety, and fear of the Lord were stirred to life in every Catholic at his or her confirmation and can manifest themselves in a number of ways. Saint Paul, while talking about the body of Christ, discusses some of the ways these gifts can be used for the good of the Christian community: for the giving of wise advice, for encouragement, for care of the sick, and for spiritual discernment. He makes it clear that these different gifts do not in any way imply that they come from different givers: "There are varieties of gifts, but the same Spirit; and there are varieties of services, but the same Lord; and there are varieties of activities, but it is the same God who activates all of them in everyone. To each is given the manifestation of the Spirit for the common good"(1 Corinthians 12:4–7).

Saint Paul wrote to the church in Corinth about this subject because they were having significant problems maintaining harmony within their Christian community. What was going on in Corinth still goes on today in campus ministries and parishes around the world. Some spiritual gifts tend to be more glamorous than others, and those who want to take on the more popular roles in a Christian community, to "clamor for the glamour," so to speak, tend to leave a sour taste in the mouths of the rest of the community. For example, many involved in campus ministry might know how to play a guitar, and there can be a tendency for people to gravitate toward leading music because of the high profile associated with that particular role in community worship. The opposite effect can be true as well. Others who have a spiritual gift or talent that doesn't seem that exciting from an outside perspective can feel as though they're not needed by a particular community and slip back into the shadows or eventually disappear from the community altogether.

What's important to recognize in a Catholic campus community, as well as in a parish community, is that there are no unnecessary parts of the body of Christ. As Saint Paul reminds us, "the members of the body that seem to be weaker are indispensable" (1 Corinthians 12:22).

How many of us know the faces, if not the names, of elderly parishioners who have arrived early to Mass every day for years without fanfare, silently interceding for the needs of their family, their parish, and the universal Church? People such as this are the contemplative engine that fuels the active Christian community.

As you're using your time in college to discern your spiritual gifts and how they'll play into your vocation, be thinking also about how those gifts fit into the landscape of not just the Church as a whole, but your community in particular. Look back on the times you've done something that seemed to come naturally to you but happened to mean a lot to a particular person in a specific situation. Maybe that took the form of your giving testimony in a group setting, leading music, offering words of encouragement, or doing a service project. And just because you happened to feel God working through you in one particular venue doesn't mean his Spirit is bound to work through you only in one specific way. Take your time as an undergraduate to develop, discern, and distribute the gifts God has given you so that you can benefit the Church and find your own sense of peace as a member of the body of Christ.

I have been blessed with these three talents:

_____

_____

_____

One natural perk of learning to recognize your own spiritual gifts and how they play into the body of Christ is that you will start to recognize God's Spirit at work in others. Someone you may have thought to be a spectator in the community might suddenly be revealed as one of its indispensable members. You may start to realize what dawned on the prophet Samuel when he was called to anoint David as the successor to King Saul: "The LORD does not see as mortals see; they

look on the outward appearance, but the LORD looks on the heart"
(1 Samuel 16:7).

What are some of your more subtle qualities that people might miss if
they don't take the time to get to know you?

_____

_____

_____

_____

   Just as no vocation can be sustained without sacrifice, no community can be sustained without it. Although the Catholic community
is there to serve your spiritual needs, it's not some magical force that
appears out of nowhere to fix your problems. A community is made
up of human beings like yourself, with similar struggles, joys, and
questions. If you find yourself benefitting from what you're receiving
from your campus ministry or parish, consider asking how you can
get involved. It's tempting to fall into one of two camps in this regard.
The first is to think of volunteering as a chance to take over some
aspect of the ministry that you find deficient and remake it in your
own image and likeness. Second, you could meekly become involved
in something in which you know your talents and gifts aren't being
best employed and stay involved for fear of disappointing someone. If
you're in the first category, chances are you have a strong personality,
and people are afraid to say anything to you because they're afraid of
the backlash they might get. If you're in the second category, chances
are you're afraid to drop out of a ministry because *you're* the one who's
afraid of the backlash. When it comes to serving God in the Catholic
community, it's not wise to let what's good get in the way of what's
best. If you feel God is calling you to a role other than the one you're
currently in, have confidence that he has prepared someone else to
assume the role you're giving up.

One of the most important things you can do for yourself on the first day you set foot on campus (even if this is your super-senior year) is to get connected with a community of Catholics, either on campus or in a local parish. Be sure not to let a sense of perfectionism limit your efforts to plug in somewhere. Sure, the music at the church nearest you may be different, the preaching might take a homily or two to get used to, and you probably won't know anyone on the first Sunday you attend. But all members of the body of Christ participate in essentially the same Mass, regardless of whether you're receiving the Eucharist in Zanesville or Zimbabwe.

If you're going to college in an area with multiple Catholic churches and no campus ministry, it can be tempting to skip from parish to parish based on your mood or preferences in a particular moment; or you might be the kind of person who hits the snooze button and keeps a list of the latest local Mass offerings on any given Sunday next to the alarm clock. If so, it's still great that you're attending Mass on a regular basis, but you're missing a key sustaining component to your formation as a Catholic college student: the ongoing engagement with a community of Catholic Christians who aren't in college. Your early days of college are a great starting point to immerse yourself in a community of people who are mostly the same age as you, traveling a spiritual path similar to yours, and primarily facing the same kinds of challenges and opportunities you're facing. And even if you choose to wait until your last semester on campus to become involved, you might be pleasantly surprised to find some strong lifelong friends there.

Staying connected to the same parish in your college years can be a form of accountability that reminds you on a tangible level that the world is made up of more than just people entering their twenties.

What things do I love best about my home parish? How can I bring what's best about the church I grew up in to the church I plan to attend while at college?

_____

_____

_____

_____

It's also important to be aware of the mentality that can develop when you start parish shopping. Focusing too much on types of worship rather than the invitation to come to our Lord's table could misguide you, as personal preferences might distract from the core of what God wants to teach you through Christ in the Eucharist. Many students who have been raised Catholic are tempted to plug into the community that tells them only the best things about themselves, feeds them the best snacks, and caters to their comfort zones. Succumbing to this mindset can open the door to a chain reaction of potential moves: when one Catholic ministry or parish doesn't satisfy you adequately, you move to another; when no Catholic parishes satisfy you adequately, you move to a nondenominational campus ministry; when no nondenominational campus ministries satisfy you, you move from one side of the pillow to the next on Sunday mornings. It may take humility and effort on your part if you want to plug into a ministry on campus or a parish close by, but in the long term, it'll be completely worth your while to make a personal investment in a consistent Catholic community.

> Various associations or movements of spiritual and apostolic life, especially those developed specifically for students, can be of great assistance in developing the pastoral aspects of university life.
>
> —*Ex Corde Ecclesiae*

An integral part of campus life is becoming involved with groups and organizations. Regardless of whether you attend a secular or a Catholic campus, a part of the tuition goes toward the support of student-led initiatives, including many that foster campus faith life. Some examples of Catholic groups one can typically find on a campus that may be under the umbrella of the campus ministry include weekly (or even daily) gatherings, prayer groups, retreats, service trips, spring-break trips, and even summer-immersion trips on some campuses. If you pay close attention, many campus ministries and Catholic universities sponsor speakers to help further your faith development. There are also men's groups, such as the Knights of Columbus and Alhambra; women's groups such as the Catholic Daughters of the Americas; vocational discernment groups for men and women; and faith households. Faith support is available on campus, and many of your greatest lifelong friendships could be made in college faith communities.

Catholic Community
at a Catholic College or University

If you're attending a Catholic college or university, the institution should be alive with Catholic identity and community promoted and supported by the local bishop(s). Although some schools are very much a work in progress in this regard, *Ex Corde Ecclesiae* specifically states that not only should Catholic universities dedicate themselves to "the cause of truth" on all levels of engagement, but campus theologians should "respect the authority of the Bishops, and assent to Catholic doctrine according to the degree of authority with which it is taught." Throughout the campus environment, the various disciplines should be united in seeking ultimate truth; and faith and reason should not be viewed as mutually exclusive but complementary and essential to each other. Considering ethics and morality in regards to everything from scientific research to the performing arts helps to develop Catholic consciousness at the university level. Are you open to researching what the Church has to say about various moral issues as your faith matures through your collegiate years? Though you wrestle with some Catholic answers, or even at first feel they are trite, engaging the question could take you on an incredible spiritual adventure.

Knowledge is not born in a vacuum, but truth is meant to connect the dots and be sought across subject lines. Thus faithful witness to this truth is not merely called for from people in specifically religious fields but is a challenge for the entire university community as well as those who seek to understand through college coursework.

Catholic campus ministries provide everyday opportunities to live out Catholic faith and morality alongside classes and extracurriculars and therefore help to integrate faith with life. Additionally, pastoral-ministry leaders should urge faculty and students to be attentive to people who are physically or spiritually hurting, such as those enduring economic, social, cultural, or religious injustices.

In general, campus life should prepare a student for life as an active adult in the Church and greater community, especially in regards to marriage and family, priestly and religious vocations, or a committed single life. All these elements of university life will be discussed later in this book.

ALUMNI DIRECTORY
Josephine Bakhita (1869–1947; born in Darfur and died in Italy)

We frequently hear about the difficulties faced by the people of Sudan. The people there have been facing hardships going back to Saint Josephine's day in the nineteenth century, and even further. Josephine was kidnapped and sold into slavery when she was only nine years old, and was then sold and resold repeatedly in the following years. In the process she was forced to endure the degrading practices that accompany the slave trade.

If faced with those kinds of situations, most of us would be tempted to become bitter and mistrusting of the entire human race, seeing every act of kindness by someone else as having an ulterior motive bent on our exploitation. However, Josephine learned that forgiveness is the path to peace, and she was eventually able to overcome the horrible mistreatment she underwent as a slave. Rather than feeling sorry for herself, she used the pain inflicted on her as motivation to reach out to others.

When she was finally bought out of slavery and given actual employment by an Italian family, her newfound Catholic faith led her to desire entry into religious life. In 1893, she did so with the Institute of Canossian Daughters of Charity, an order she was a part of for the remaining nearly fifty years of her life. Though before she had been isolated from community and interaction with the rest of society as a slave, she learned to overcome the hardships of her former life and integrate into Christian community in a profound way, becoming an advocate for the poor and the sick. She also became a much-sought-after speaker as a result of her missionary work. She even had a starring role in Pope Benedict's encyclical *Spe Salvi,* or as it's titled in English, *Saved in Hope.* Saint Josephine could have descended into despair due to her difficulties with integration into a community, but she persevered and is now a powerful intercessor in the kingdom.

MEMORY VERSE

"Day by day, as they spent much time together in the temple, they broke bread at home and ate their food with glad and generous hearts, praising God and having the goodwill of all the people. And day by day the Lord added to their number those who were being saved" (Acts 2:46–47).

CATECHISM OF THE CATHOLIC CHURCH
Love of Neighbor

The "fraternity" discussed in this section of the *Catechism* isn't your garden-variety men's campus organization but the shared impulse toward an objective.

"There is a certain resemblance between the unity of the divine persons and the fraternity that men are to establish among themselves in truth and love. Love of neighbor is inseparable from love of God" (*CCC* 1878).

Which do you find more difficult to spend time working on: love of neighbor (friends, family, acquaintances, people on social media you can't remember how you know, professors, or that person who always leaves dirty dishes in your dorm's hall kitchen) or love of God? How so?

_____

_____

_____

_____

Do you tend to love yourself more than your neighbor or God? Do you tend to love yourself less than you love your neighbor or God? Explain.

_____

_____

_____

EXTRA CREDIT
Practical Steps Toward Finding Catholic Community

- Even before moving on campus, visit your college's website, masstimes.org, or the website of the diocese in which you plan to attend school, and figure out your options for Sunday Mass. It's OK if it takes you a few tries to decide which local parish is home, but when you find a parish home, try to stick to it. Cancel or postpone other obligations if necessary to stay connected with that parish, even if you go to the Saturday vigil Mass one week and the Sunday 11:00 AM Mass the next. You might be surprised to know that many campuses offer student Masses on Sunday evenings as well. Find another student in your dormitory and make a habit of going to Mass together.

- Pick up a parish bulletin at the church where you plan to consistently attend, or check out your Catholic campus ministry's website. Scan it for ministries that appeal to your interests, gifts, and talents. Take a look at your school's activity schedule and see if it's possible to devote an hour weekly, biweekly or monthly to some parish- or campus-ministry–related cause.

- Meet with your campus's Catholic chaplain or call the parish office of the church you plan to attend, introducing yourself to the pastor, campus minister(s), and parish secretary. Let them know who you are, and give them a quick rundown of your background. You'll be surprised at how well they'll remember your name and face from this simple act.

SUGGESTED READING

- *The Temperament God Gave You* by Art and Laraine Bennett. Everyone's personality has its positive and negative aspects, and every personality can be valuable to the wider Catholic community in some way. The Bennetts help readers figure out where their personalities fall in the mix, and how those personalities can be best integrated into the broader mission of the Church.

- *Should I Become a Cantor?* and *Should I Become a Lector?* by Charlene Altemose. These are two of the more high-profile ways you can share your gifts in the liturgy, yet these two pamphlets might get you to start thinking about how your gifts can be of wider service to your parish.

- *Forming Intentional Disciples* by Sherry Weddell. Weddell digs into the reasons people stay connected with their parish and the reasons they leave, what parishioners are looking for in a church, and how to meet the needs of the average Catholic in the pew. Understanding what may be drawing you toward or away from parish life might help you find ways to more intentionally make participation in Catholic community a part of your college experience.

PRAYER

Father, thank you for blessing your people with the gift of Christian community. Lead me to become a vital part of the Catholic community on campus through involvement with other young adults ready to serve you in parish life.

Give me a boldness for sharing in fellowship opportunities by reaching out in goodwill to students who likewise share the faith. Make me willing to serve as a support to other believers on campus as an extension of my parish family back home.

I ask this through your Son, Jesus Christ. Amen.

Living Service in the Light of Catholic Social Teaching

It is necessary to foster a culture of acceptance, respect and sharing, while remembering that "man can fully discover his true self only in a sincere giving of himself" (*Gaudium et Spes*, 24) by committing his own freedom to the common good, beyond individual or group interests and far from the search for profit at all costs.

POPE JOHN PAUL II, MAY 5, 2000,
MESSAGE OF THE HOLY FATHER TO THE
CATHOLIC UNIVERSITY OF THE SACRED HEART

University life is a bit strange because, while on a college campus, you'll have the opportunity to engage with people of other cultures and to seek out knowledge from diverse origins. You'll also find yourself in a situation where you're living and working with people who are all about the same age as you, a circumstance not likely to happen again in this same way. These experiences can be wonderful and challenging, but they can also cause you to forget what it's like to live outside the young-adult bubble, making you a bit immune to the scenarios people outside the world of academics face. And when you mix all of this with a little apathy, college can become an extremely self-centered time, but it doesn't have to be.

G. K. Chesterton once said that "children are innocent and love *justice*; while most of us are wicked and naturally prefer *mercy*." All of us struggle with the balance of justice and mercy in our lives. We want to see the wrongs others have committed to be corrected, and we want our own sins to be forgiven. After diligent research of the social issues, hopefully you will be inspired to combat apathy and seek action of some sort. Not only will charitable work benefit others, but it will be of inestimable value to your own well-being, especially if you're feeling badly about yourself, your situation, or even a little bit down. Getting out and doing for others, or better yet, teaming up with college students like yourself, will get you out of your own head while widening your horizons about the larger world out there. You might even be surprised to find that many sufferings happen in your own backyard.

What are some cases of injustice that you have learned more about in the last couple of years? Have you done anything to alleviate these sufferings?

_____

_____

_____

_____

_____

_____

As a Catholic, it can be hard to determine which injustices most warrant your attention. Some Catholic thinkers have advocated, and rightly so, the idea of a "seamless garment"; that is, the idea that we shouldn't let our defense of the unborn or the elderly interfere with our responsibility to speak out on other issues, such as war, poverty, or the death penalty. However, the "seamless garment" argument can also be misrepresented as meaning that things like abortion, euthanasia, war, the death penalty, and other issues all hold the same moral weight. In these first days of college, you'll be assaulted with all kinds of social issues that people believe need to be corrected, and it's crucial to practice discernment as to which of them truly are social evils and deserve your best efforts. This is where the wisdom of the Church can lend a helping hand.

From its very beginnings, the Church has had a radical hand in what is known as social justice. Catholic social teaching concerns itself with the welfare of all people: health care for the poor, feeding the hungry, defending the rights of the worker, and advocating respect for the elderly and the unborn are all areas in which Catholics have led the way throughout history. With so many needs and so little time and money on a college schedule and a college budget, it can be difficult to discern the specific kind of social work best suited to our gifts, talents, and the moral priorities of a given time and place.

For starters, it may be helpful to reference the *Catechism* to discover and define underlying principles for social justice as taught by our faith. According to the Church, "respect for the human person proceeds by way of respect for the principle that everyone should look upon his neighbor (without any exception) as 'another self'" (*CCC* 1931).

What, then, does it mean that we should look upon each of our neighbors as another self? In the Gospel of Matthew, Jesus tells us, "'You shall love the Lord your God with all your heart, and with all your soul, and with all your mind.' This is the greatest and first commandment. And a second is like it: 'You shall love your neighbor as yourself'" (22:37–39).

This passage has many implications, one of which is that if you don't love yourself, it will be hard to love your neighbor. Another question Jesus raises in this teaching is, What does love of neighbor even look like? Does love mean never being critical of people's beliefs or actions, constantly being critical of people's beliefs and actions, or something significantly more complicated? In your first days of college, you'll be confronted with a host of causes and opinions in regard to social justice, and it will be crucial to figure out where all of them fit into the grand scheme of things so that you can determine where to most effectively steer your efforts, especially in light of your own God-given gifts.

To be sure, not all social injustices hold the same moral weight. Obviously, murdering the unborn or starving an elderly or disabled person to death come with far more serious consequences than other worthy causes such as recycling or adopting abused pets. This is not to say the latter aren't important. We just have to remember, as the *Catechism* teaches, that social justice is respecting the dignity of all humanity—that is, the eternal and transcendent nature of the people of God. Given that criteria, we can at least take a stab at understanding how legitimate social-justice causes are worthy of our time and energy but vary in their gravity.

Perhaps there are Catholic-friendly groups on your campus that are focused on the pro-life movement. These can be great organizations to tap into. Some may be Catholic, while others might provide you an opportunity to work in common with other faith communities, Christian and non-Christian alike. Don't miss these opportunities if at all possible, since defense of the weakest and most voiceless among us is one of the highest priorities when it comes to social justice. Also, getting involved in these primary social-justice issues can lead to other great opportunities in regard to volunteerism and other efforts. For example, learning about the inherent connection between human trafficking and abortion can encourage you to participate in organizations that combat that particular social evil. Learning the rates of abortion among the poverty stricken could lead you to participate in an anti-poverty program. Anti-poverty programs may actually be the easiest way to get involved in social-justice efforts, since organizations like The Society for St. Vincent de Paul are constantly looking for volunteers.

You may find that the social-justice organizations to which your priorities are most inclined are already well staffed and that God might be calling you to participate in a social concern that happens to fly below the radar of the general public. Maybe you can give time weekly to an underprivileged-youth sports camp or become involved in efforts to collect school supplies for children who can't afford them.

Although some social-justice efforts operate year round, fall and spring break can provide unique opportunities to do something more focused, short term, and immersive. Contact the Mission Office of your campus ministry about opportunities to use your spring break in service to the poor either domestically or internationally. Having the opportunity to meet people from different cultural backgrounds and see the faith of those who have so much less than the average middle-class family could move your heart in ways you would never have expected. Who knows, perhaps you will even be called to serve through mission work in your life either here or abroad.

When I [Matt] was in college, I had the opportunity to use one of my spring breaks to do a week-long mission with the Christian Appalachian Project (CAP). When the late Msgr. Ralph Beiting was sent to Eastern Kentucky in 1950, his parish responsibilities covered several counties, and at that time only a tiny percentage of the population was Catholic. After seeing the great poverty of so many of the Appalachian people, he founded CAP to provide food, medicine, housing, and educational opportunities for the poor, whether they were Catholic or not. In many cases, these people were cut off from the medical and technological progress being enjoyed across the rest of the United States. Through his dedication to the least among us, his ministry grew and eventually even attracted the assistance of non-Catholics from across the country. Every year, numerous work weeks are available through CAP and are offered specifically to college students, who can participate in everything from building new roofs for battered homes to teaching literacy to students and adults alike. In my case, this was a life-changing experience that I'll always remember, and one that I found out about by asking the head of my college's social-work department.

These types of programs are often developed particularly to give college students a taste for service during these years when you are learning so many things. If you find you enjoy service and justice work, you could continue to serve post-college as well. Sometimes these post-college service programs will offer to pay down student loans in exchange for being involved with their organizations for a set number of years. If this is something that appeals to your instincts and gifts, look up the closest representative from the Jesuit Volunteer Corps, Lay Salesian Missioners, or other similar groups and see if this is the kind of work for which God may be calling you, even if it is just for a short time after college.

Giving Even When You Are Broke

It may sound like a crazy idea to commit part of your strapped college budget to making a weekly gift at your parish, but you'd be surprised at how this simple gesture can reorient your ideas toward stewardship. Recall the scene in Luke 21:1–4, when Jesus witnessed rich temple patrons putting in large amounts of money that were a drop in the financial bucket for them and then witnessed a poor widow throwing a couple of coins in the coffer. For a millionaire, a few thousand bucks doesn't constitute sacrifice, but for a hundredaire or a dozenaire as is likely the case for you, a couple of bucks might not seem like much in the grand scheme of things when the baskets are passed at Mass. However, the very act of giving something is evidence that you're willing to prioritize your spending toward a sacrificial end, even if you're the only one who knows the kind of sacrifice you're making.

If you grew up in a parish that participated in Catholic Relief Services' (CRS) Operation Rice Bowl program, you know the impact a few pennies can have toward making foodstuffs available to people surviving on far less than the average college-student's budget. Ten dollars may barely buy two value meals at the local fast-food chain, but that same amount of money can feed a family of six far hungrier than you through CRS Rice Bowl. Keeping a change jar year round and not just during Lent when this program is highlighted can help you to stay consciously aware of the needs of others, even if you have to fish out a couple of quarters every now and then to buy some microwave popcorn during an all-night study session.

Have you given money to your parish or to other charitable organizations over the years, either out of your own allowance or from the money you made from jobs you had while in high school? If so, which organizations did you support? What did you learn through the course of making those sacrifices?

_____

_____

_____

_____

Another way in which you might think about being generous with your limited resources is when you go to sell back your books. Granted, you might be getting back way less cash than you paid out initially, but for a college student with limited resources, sell-back day can be like Christmas. Consider committing 10 percent of the money you receive from selling back your books to a particular charity or to your parish. As one of the few times during the school year when you experience a tiny bit of a windfall, it's great to remember to bless others, just as you've been briefly blessed in a small way.

And finally, when it comes to making financial sacrifices, which benefit not only the recipients of your sacrifices but also your own maturing sense of charity, it's important to remember the words of Saint Paul: "Brothers and sisters: the one who sows sparingly will also reap sparingly, and the one who sows bountifully will also reap bountifully. Each of you must give as you have made up your mind, not reluctantly or under compulsion, for God loves a cheerful giver" (2 Corinthians 9:6–7).

Who are some of the people in your life who have been the greatest examples of generosity? What was their attitude toward giving money, time, or energy?

_____

_____

_____

_____

ALUMNI DIRECTORY
Blessed Pier Giorgio Frassati (1901–1925; Turin, Italy)

From all outward appearances, Blessed Pier Giorgio Frassati could have lived his life comfortably without doing anything for anyone but himself and gotten away with it. He was born into a wealthy and politically influential twentieth-century Italian family. And he was handsome, charismatic, athletic, and good at almost everything he tried to do. Frassati was popular among his peers, notorious for his good-natured practical jokes, and highly intelligent, entering a prestigious engineering program just out of high school.

It could have been easy for someone born into this kind of charmed life to ignore God and focus only on his own talents, interests, and aspirations, but Pier Giorgio was cut from a different cloth. In addition to making time for things like mountain climbing and skiing with friends, he also made time for Eucharistic Adoration, volunteer work with the poor and the sick, and Catholic Action, an organization that opposed the oppressive goals of Fascism in Italy between the First and Second World Wars.

Pier Giorgio was so devoted to working closely with the impoverished and the ill that he eventually contracted polio and died. Nobody required him to give of himself so sacrificially to those less fortunate than him; but through his own close connection with the sacraments, he knew the importance of bringing the Christ he received in the Eucharist to those who most needed the healing presence of the Lord

During the International Jubilee for Athletes in 1984, Blessed Pope John Paul II said:

"Pier Giorgio…was a modern young man open to the values of sport—he was a skillful mountaineer and able skier—but at the same time he bore a courageous witness of generosity in Christian faith and charity toward others, especially the very poor and the suffering. The Lord called him to himself at only twenty-four years of age, in July 1925, but he is still very much alive among us with his smile and his goodness, inviting his contemporaries to the love of Christ and a virtuous life. After the First World War he wrote the following: 'Through charity, peace is sown among men, not the peace that the world gives but the true peace that only faith in Christ can give us, making us brothers and sisters.'"

MEMORY VERSE

"What good is it, my brothers and sisters, if you say you have faith but do not have works? Can faith save you? If a brother or sister is naked and lacks daily food, and one of you says to them, 'Go in peace; keep warm and eat your fill,' and yet you do not supply their bodily needs, what is the good of that? So faith by itself, if it has no works, is dead" (James 2:14–17).

Are you more faith-heavy, works-heavy, or do you have a good balance of both? Explain.

_____

_____

_____

_____

_____

_____

CATECHISM OF THE CATHOLIC CHURCH
Respect, Charity, and Solidarity

"Respect for the human person entails respect for the rights that flow from his dignity as a creature. These rights are prior to society and must be recognized by it" (*CCC* 1930).

"The differences among persons belong to God's plan, who wills that we should need one another. These differences should encourage charity" (*CCC* 1946).

"Solidarity is an eminently Christian virtue. It practices the sharing of spiritual goods even more than material ones" (*CCC* 1948).

SUGGESTED READING

- *Loaves and Fishes* by Dorothy Day. Dorothy Day shattered the conventions of her age in a number of ways. A former Communist and post-abortive mother who had a radical conversion to Catholicism while working with poor immigrants in New York, she understood the balance of radical commitment to the sacraments and radical commitment to the least among us. Her faithful Catholic testimony serves as a challenge to the polarized political climates that dominate and distort the global conversation about social justice.

- *Something Beautiful for God* by Malcolm Muggeridge. Many of us have heard of the powerful witness of Mother Teresa of Calcutta, but it's unclear how widely known her story would be today had it not been chronicled by Malcolm Muggeridge, a previously agnostic journalist and satirist whose life was transformed by witnessing the work of the Missionaries of Charity in Calcutta, India, and Mother Teresa's witness in particular. His account of her life of sacrifice and charity is evidence of the impact that selfless commitment to Christ's call to serve the least among us can inspire in others and even convert their hearts.

- *Caritas in Veritate* by Pope Benedict XVI. In his third encyclical letter as pope, Benedict writes: "[Charity] gives real substance to the personal relationship with God and with neighbor; it is the principle not only of micro-relationships (with friends, with family members or within small groups) but also of macro-relationships (social, economic and political ones)" (2). The Holy Father explores the implications of social justice not only when it comes to the neighbors we meet face-to-face in our daily encounters, but also in regard to those neighbors in the global human family whom we may never meet.

Extra Credit
Practical Steps Toward Realizing the Call

- Ask your local Catholic campus minister about volunteer opportunities available in your area. Find a Catholic classmate with whom you can partner to work with one of the organizations you both connect with, and keep each other accountable to participate regularly in the mission of that particular apostolate.

- Spend some time in Eucharistic Adoration, asking our Lord how he's asking you to use your gifts and talents to advance the social mission of the Church. Take a list of the organizations you're interested in and present them to Jesus before the Blessed Sacrament. Clear your mind by listening for God's direction as to where your gifts and talents might be best applied.

- Set aside a change jar, even if you only deposit excess pennies in it. Label it so that you can distinguish it from the rest of your limited cash reserves, and designate it specifically for charitable stewardship.

- Contact your campus ministry or your local diocese for mission opportunities and see what special programs they have available for short-term mission trips specifically geared to college students. Some of these opportunities provide fundraising or are sponsored, which means there's less pressure on you when it comes to providing funds for the trip. Block out one spring break during your time in college and dedicate it toward a short-term mission trip. If you happen to know what opportunities are out there, research the area where you intend to go. It might also help to keep a journal and say regular prayers for the people you'll be helping as the trip approaches.

PRAYER

"Make us worthy, Lord, to serve our fellow-men throughout the world who live and die in poverty and hunger. Give them through our hands this day their daily bread, and by our understanding love, give peace and joy."

POPE PAUL VI

6

24/7: Balancing It All With So Many Available Options

Building your own lives and building society are not tasks that can be accomplished by distracted or superficial minds and hearts. They require profound educational action and continuous discernment that must involve the whole of the academic community, encouraging that synthesis between intellectual formation, moral discipline and religious commitment which Bl. John Henry Newman proposed in his *The Idea of a University.*

POPE BENEDICT XVI, DECEMBER 16, 2010,
CELEBRATION OF VESPERS WITH UNIVERSITY STUDENTS
AND TEACHERS OF ROME

Why It's Important to Take This Chapter Seriously

One of the great things about dorm life is the opportunity to make new friendships and form new bonds, possibly with different types of people than you might have naturally gravitated toward in high school. Being thrown into a living situation with a variety of different people with various backgrounds, interests, and worldviews will give you an opportunity to expand your understanding as to the kind of people that make up the world. Because of the shared experiences that dorm life provides, you may find yourself forging closer bonds with the people you live with for four years in college than you did with people you may have gone to school with up to twelve years prior. Whether you had a largely positive or negative experience of high school, chances are you'll end up defining yourself more by what went on in your college years ten years after graduation.

In 140 characters or less, express your hopes for your college experience.

_____

_____

_____

_____

Part of this defining process comes from what may seem to be insignificant shared experiences, such as staying up late in a study group with a couple of people who share a class with you or cramming into someone's room to watch a movie or an athletic event. Some, however, will be much more significant, such as staying up *ridiculously* late discussing relationships, personal struggles, or faith issues. It may not have been possible to stay up until 2:00 AM with a high school classmate on a Tuesday night eating pizza and talking philosophy, but in college these kinds of opportunities are far more common. As Venerable Archbishop Fulton J. Sheen once said, the faith is more "caught" than "taught." Use these bonding opportunities as a chance to let your lived experience of the love of Christ and what he's done for you show so that when someone who's bonded with you needs support at midnight on a weekday, you can offer them some small part of the peace you've hopefully received through your relationship with Jesus. In my own experience, sometimes these conversations did not even happen until after college, but the bonds forged in dorm and college life so very often lay the groundwork that makes friends feel comfortable contacting another about spiritual matters a few years down the road.

Many of the friendships you form with your dorm or housemates will stick with you for decades. You may be out of touch with some of these friends for years, but as soon as you run into them again, it'll feel almost like you're back in the dorms, sorting out how much money each of you has to throw in for a pizza. You'll watch these friends get married and have children, and in a social-media age, track them through the ups and downs of their adult life. As you wonder at the experience of living on campus, try to identify the ways in which the bonds you form in community life as a college student differ from the bonds you formed in high school. Once again, this drives home the importance of making sure that the core relationships you develop at the beginning of your college experience are ones with people who share your values and who will support you in your efforts to live them.

If you do decide to live on campus, and I highly recommend it for as long as it's financially feasible, you will be hit between the eyes with a whole new set of responsibilities. Some of these will be new versions of old responsibilities, such as organizing your laundry or doing your homework. However, some of them will be new ones, such as taking care of every single meal you eat while you're at school. Study after study has shown that in their first semester, a large number of students either gain or lose weight, often because they're learning how to feed themselves for the first time. Some people who have been fed healthy meals by their parents begin eating cheeseburgers or sugary cereals for every meal, while others who are used to being waited on hand and foot by their parents become paralyzed by their inability to feed themselves and forget to eat altogether.

Another very important responsibility to manage while in college involves making and maintaining a budget. Few college students are seasoned in this area, especially if one's parents have taken care of all their essential and recreational needs prior to their leaving for school. It can be very easy to blow an entire month's supply of cash on fast food and entertainment in the course of a few days. Add to that the presence of a potential host of dorm mates with more privileged financial backgrounds who might not be exercising fiscal prudence but have a seemingly unending stream of cash flow thrown at them by their parents. By watching others, you might find the temptation to be irresponsible with your money even more enticing. If every night of the week after the campus cafeteria is closed, someone on your hall wants to throw in a few bucks for a pizza and watch a movie, you could feel like an outsider if you don't get out your wallet.

It's also easy to get technologically envious of other people in your campus housing who have bigger-screen TVs, better surround sound, nicer MP3 players, and more advanced smartphones than you do. Some college students are already living the American dream in their dorm room without ever having had to work for it. Some of the students in your dorms may have been mowing lawns for cash since they were twelve, but some may be planning to enter the world of employment for the first time after graduation. Don't get caught up in the need to spend money to keep up with them. Put together a budget that takes into account your needs in regard to toiletries, transportation, snacks, entertainment, and whatever other necessities you know will require cash. If you can, secure some kind of employment that doesn't interfere with your academics (such as a work-study position if you qualify) so that you can begin to take responsibility for funding your own campus experience and make the transition toward financial independence once you're no longer under your parents' economic umbrella. You may not be able to do every single fun thing every single time it's presented to you, but you'll begin to gain a greater appreciation for the things you *are* able to do because you've earned them.

Finally, when it comes to taking on responsibility as a college student, one of the hardest areas to manage is one's use of time. If staying up late was a temptation before, it'll be significantly more tempting now. And if video games caused you to lose hours at a time in high school, get ready for them to become even more of a potential time waster. If you had a tendency to text when you should have been studying, that temptation will manifest itself more than ever once you get to college. Nobody will be looking over your shoulder and telling you that you should be working on a paper instead of checking your social network, and nobody will be waking you when you sleep through your alarm. It's up to you to ensure that you make the best use of your time. Whereas you might have come from a living situation where the tone was set by a parent or guardian twenty or more years older than you, now you'll be living in a place where the tone is set by people the same age as you, many of them trying to figure out how to live by themselves and independently manage their obligations for the first time just like you are.

Try posting a schedule in your room that reminds you that checking social media might be fun, but you need to unplug at a certain time each day for a set period before you can log back on. Though it can be tempting to put off homework to watch a movie, try to reward yourself with a movie or TV show after you've accomplished a task you'd rather put off. Otherwise, you'll frequently find yourself writing entire papers at 3:00 AM (or later!) on the day they're due.

Many young people are at university, which enables them to broaden their horizons, to be passionately involved in scientific research and to deepen their reflection on various aspects of the complexities of human life. It is essential that they be made aware that they live in a world shaped by the previous generations which demands from each one of them the creative contribution of a mature personality, serious commitment to research and original thought.—Letter of Cardinal Angelo Sodano to Cardinal Dionigi Tettamanzi on the Occasion of the 80th "Day for the Catholic University of the Sacred Heart," April 25, 2004

Speaking of papers, whether you're a student athlete or just playing an epic amount of video games, the academic life has to factor somehow into the reason you went to college in the first place. With a fast-paced social schedule, challenges to live healthily, budgetary constraints, a disciplined spiritual life, and worthy causes in which to take part, it can be difficult to focus on one's studies. When everything seems to be clamoring for your attention at once, the ideal goal of bettering yourself academically and intellectually can start to seem not only impractical, but impossible. It is precisely at these moments that we need to know how to handle the stresses of daily living and use our study time effectively; and believe it or not, the self-control you've had to practice and live by as a morally upright follower of Christ will serve you well, because being disciplined in your life of virtue and faith will reflect positively in the attention you're able to place on your studies.

When you stop and think about all the ways we humans can possibly spend our allotted twenty-four hours a day, it's staggering, especially on a breakneck college schedule. Not only are there a plethora of activities going on around campus vying for our attention, but the very tools we use to stay organized—our smartphones, tablets, and laptops—can also become our biggest enemies against time if we're not careful. Due to the fact that inattention is one of the biggest struggles of the contemporary student, not to mention working professionals, family units, and so forth, we need to practice focus daily to get even close to mastering it. As Christians, we're not called to a life of chaos and confusion, but to life in Christ. That means zeroing in on the major task at hand in college—studies—and finding ways to seek truth in the best possible way. Although it's no secret that we're all juggling an assortment of responsibilities while in college and beyond, it's all right to question the contemporary world's fascination with multitasking, especially when it comes to buckling down and studying. You're going to have to find the study methods that work best for your individual personality type, but we can't stress enough how much liberty can be found in breaking free from your tech and cracking the books.

This doesn't necessarily mean not staying plugged in to a certain degree. One of the reasons I'm so fond of my e-reader, as opposed to reading an e-text on my laptop or smartphone or even a tablet, is that aside from the lack of glare and eye strain, my abilities to procrastinate are rather limited. I know myself, and knowing myself means being aware that focus doesn't come easy. When I need to really get down to work, managing my environment and keeping distractions to a minimum are key. That means seeking out a quiet place, such as a campus library or lawn, and putting my phone on silent and out of sight. The type of in-depth reading assignments required in nearly every collegiate department aren't going to be mastered by answering a text mid-paragraph, even if you answer from the depths of a library study cubicle. Staying socially on-call while studying will make your study sessions last at least twice as long and will certainly have an effect on your attentiveness and the depth to which you can understand the assignment at hand, thus making the material you're studying difficult to retain. Study at a leisurely pace in a place that allows you to work relatively free from distractions. For the most part, this is not your dormitory lounge or even your dorm room. That way, when you are ready to kick back and relax or spend time with friends, you can do it relatively stress and guilt-free, knowing you used your study time effectively.

Once you really start getting into your chosen discipline, you'll find that the more you know, the more you realize you don't know. This can be humbling and exciting all at the same time, especially when you realize that this phenomena will pretty much never go away if you plan on being a lifelong learner (which I hope you do!). Although it will be important to pay your bills once you've gotten out of college and into your chosen career, make sure you're genuinely interested in what you are studying and your career path. Getting to class on time and sitting somewhere that will be most advantageous for your learning needs are key, although some of you may have trouble even getting to class at all. Sitting at the front of the classroom will help you stay focused, keeping you accountable against the tendency to zone out or cruise your social-media network of choice. Remember, you will want to use your tuition dollars in the wisest way possible since you'll likely be paying the interest on them for more than a couple of years once you leave school. Taking small steps to increase your in-class engagement will also allow you to feel more comfortable asking questions when the material needs clarification or you've got another sort of question or comment related to a classroom discussion.

On a very related note, in addition to your studies, make time every day for leisure, rest, physical exercise, and spiritual reading and prayer. Monks are the original academics, and one of the important lessons that monastic life can teach us is that an ordered day is a productive and balanced one. College is going to present a wide range of surprises, joys, trials, and struggles. Give yourself a good head start by taking care of the basics to the best of your ability.

For some of you, that might mean making an extra effort to keep your dorm room clean so that when it comes time to write that six-page paper on Plato's Cave, you've already got a nice work environment and one less reason to procrastinate. For others, it might mean setting your alarm clock so that you're awake for more daylight hours and getting a better and more ordered sleep so that you are less likely to be sweating to make it to class on time. And still others might need to spend more time exercising your body at the campus recreation center by attending classes, swimming, or joining intramural sports teams.

ALUMNI DIRECTORY
Edith Stein, aka Saint Teresa Benedicta of the Cross
(1891–1942; born Wroclaw, Poland, and died in
Auschwitz concentration camp)

Born into a Jewish family in nineteenth-century Germany, Edith lost interest in her faith during her early teenage years. For her collegiate program, she studied philosophy, and specifically the field of phenomenology, which is the study of experience and consciousness. Her quest for the truth, combined with her friendships with faithful Catholics, eventually led her to convert to Catholicism in 1925.

Edith's pursuit of knowledge in the discipline of philosophy led her to explore and eventually find God. As a young Catholic, this discernment process led her to follow a call to the religious life. Following in the footsteps of one of her heroes, Saint Teresa of Avila, she joined the Carmelite order and embraced a lifestyle that was both academically and spiritually rigorous. In honor of Saint Teresa, she took the religious name Saint Teresa Benedicta of the Cross.

Unfortunately, because she was at the same time Jewish, Catholic, outspoken, and articulate, the Nazis knew exactly how to track her down when they took control of the government. She was smuggled out of Germany to the Netherlands to avoid being taken away to a German death camp. When the Dutch bishops spoke out as one against the racist ideologies of the Nazis, Hitler's army retaliated by targeting Dutch Catholics, and Saint Teresa was among those arrested. Along with her sister, Rose, she was eventually gassed in the concentration camps of Auschwitz.

Saint Teresa Benedicta knew it was important to balance high-minded philosophical discussions by engaging the culture of her present day. She had to wrestle not only with the ideas of the long-dead minds she was studying but with those present-minded falsehoods of the people who were overhauling Eastern Europe during the course of her lifetime. If she had only focused on the circumstances of her plight as a potential victim of Hitler's regime, we might easily have forgotten her name, but because she was able to balance her view toward eternity with her view of the present moment, her reflections on the meaning of our existence are still applicable to the present day. In fact, Blessed Pope John Paul II, who endured persecution from the Nazis and eventually helped to defeat Communism, considered Saint Teresa Benedicta of the Cross one of his greatest intellectual influences.

MEMORY VERSE

"Wisdom is radiant and unfading, and she is easily discerned by those who love her, and is found by those who seek her" (Wisdom 6:12).

What is your primary motivation for going to college? Do you intend to acquire wisdom, or something else? How is wisdom different from knowledge?

_____

_____

_____

_____

_____

_____

CATECHISM OF THE CATHOLIC CHURCH
Human Freedom

"Human freedom is a force for growth and maturity in truth and goodness; it attains its perfection when directed toward God, our beatitude" (*CCC* 1731).

SUGGESTED READING

- *Disorientation: How to Go to College Without Losing Your Mind* by Peter Kreeft, Donna Steichen, George Rutler, Eric Metaxas, and others. Though you might not face the kinds of life-and-death struggles that Edith Stein had to face in sorting out the philosophies of her age, you'll still have to deal with things like relativism, hedonism, secularism, and postmodernism, which will all vie for your attention. This book features a series of Catholic thinkers who can help you spot subversive philosophies hostile to your Catholic faith, whether they happen to surface in a classroom, dorm, or coffeehouse.

- *Faith Bound: Prayers By and 4 College Students:* A Redemptorist Pastoral Publication. Covering a range of concerns from time management to vocational discernment to interaction with peers, this collection of prayers specifically geared toward the concerns of college students can be a great help when you can't find the way to put your own feelings into words, especially given the wide spectrum of challenges and opportunities you'll face in college.

- *Spiritual Blueprint: How We Live, Work, Love, Play, and Pray* by James Papandrea, PhD. Papandrea takes an extremely practical approach when it comes to analyzing the ways our faith should influence our lives in regard to vocation, relationships, and spirituality. Built as a workbook, he sets up thought-provoking questions about who you are and how you're balancing God's call in your everyday routine so that you can take a sort of inventory as to how you're using your time, talents, and treasures, thus enabling you to consider using them wisely.

Extra Credit
Practical Steps Toward Living Christian Ethics

- For one day, document how you spend your time, paying careful attention to serial time wasters. Make a timeline, and try to be conscious about dedicating blocks of time to your efforts rather than taking the multitasking route where you check your social networks after every paragraph you write for your research paper. Do the math and see what's positive about your daily schedule and what you'd like to improve.

- Inspired by the original academics, the monastics, create a rule of life. That is, an ideal daily schedule that accounts for all basic needs: nourishment, sleep, leisure, study time, physical activity, spiritual reading, and prayer. Create your own rule and see if any daily stresses are relieved. After a day or two of trying it out, make adjustments as needed.

- If you have a smartphone that will allow you to program multiple alarms, set timers to remind you of specific points in the day when you should study, pray, take leisure time, or even read books that aren't on your academic reading list. Stick to that schedule as diligently as you can; if you lose track of time, don't give up, but keep those notifications armed so that you can try to do better the next day.

Prayer

God grant me the serenity to
accept the things I cannot change;
courage to change the things I can;
and wisdom to know the difference.

Realizing the Call:
Vocational Discernment
and Holiness for All

Then Peter said, "Look, we have left our homes and followed you."
And [Jesus] said to them, "Truly I tell you, there is no one who has
left house or wife or brothers or parents or children, for the sake
of the kingdom of God, who will not get back very much more in
this age, and in the age to come eternal life."

LUKE 18:28–30

Every person has a vocation. You may have heard your parish engaging
in prayers for vocations at Mass or other events and assumed that the
only people who have vocations are priests and religious. In reality,
you have a vocation, even if you aren't called to the priesthood or religious life. Marriage is a vocation, as is the life of a single person who
is committed to the service of others. Your vocation isn't about what
you do for a living; that's a secondary call. Rather, it's about the state
of life God has planned for you as the clearest path toward sanctity
and, ultimately, eternal life.

With that in mind, college is an important time to focus on your major and potential career path, but it's equally important to remember that these aims are hollow if they're pursued at the expense of one's true path to holiness. Your college experience may launch you into a lucrative career in law, medicine, or engineering, but as Jesus himself asks, "For what will it profit them to gain the whole world and forfeit their life?" (Mark 8:36).

At this point, what is your declared major, or what do you plan on declaring as your major? How about your minor(s)? How might they fit into life as a priest, religious, spouse, missionary, and so forth?

_____

_____

_____

_____

_____

_____

Why It's Important to Take This Chapter Seriously

Ask the married people you know when and how they met. How many of them met in college or through a college friend? Ask the priests you know when they started seminary, or male or female religious when they started as novices in their order. How many of them began that journey either during their college years or shortly after? You're at a unique crossroads in life, where you're transitioning out of being cared for by others and into the opportunity to care for yourself and others to a greater degree. It's especially important during your college years to listen to how God is calling you to serve, not just in a profession, but in a vocation as well.

Think of the married couple you look up to most. Where and how did they meet? If you don't know and have the opportunity, ask them their story.

_____

_____

_____

_____

The *Catechism* refers to the sacraments of holy orders and matrimony as "Sacraments at the Service of Communion," meaning, as it puts it, that they are "directed towards the salvation of others" (*CCC* 1534). Your baptism, confirmation, Communion, and reconciliation are all directed toward your own salvation; baptism initiates you into the Church, confirmation seals your baptism, and you are continually renewed and connected with Christ through the Eucharist and confession. But marriage and holy orders are different; they're directed outward rather than inward. That means when two people participate in the sacrament of matrimony, they are vowing to sacrifice themselves to help their spouse make it to heaven, just as a priest, when he undergoes the rite of ordination, is vowing to sacrifice himself to help his flock get to heaven. The same is true of religious sisters and brothers, as well as those committed or consecrated to a chaste single life; your life is not your own but, rather belongs to Christ for him to do with it what he will through whatever state of life he's called you to embrace.

Regarding the single life, there may be a temptation, even among college students, to assume they have what might be regarded as a transitional vocation to the single life. This is to say that they don't feel comfortable attaching themselves to any vocation in particular anytime soon. If you go around telling people you think you have a vocation to the single life, ask yourself, *Am I ready to make a private lifelong vow of consecrated virginity?* My guess is probably not!

God doesn't call people to the single life so that they can rent movies and play video games during all of their free time. Some of the saints who embraced the single life include Saint Giuseppe Moscato, who devoted his life to working with the sick at all hours of the day until he contracted a disease and died in his thirties; Saint Agnes, who was a virgin martyr as a young teenager; and Saint Francis of Assisi, who contrary to popular belief was not a priest but a brother and permanent deacon. The vocation to the single life still requires self-sacrifice, since all vocations are ordered toward service.

Marriage is the vocation to which most people, as a rule, are called. Even in a culture that oftentimes seems to place a low value on the idea of a lifelong sacramental bond between a man and a woman, there is still an idea voiced in movies and music that love should be forever and that growing old together is a good thing. Hollywood marriages may last only a couple of years on average, but at least Hollywood culture acknowledges that there is something about marriage that is qualitatively different than just living with your significant other, even if it gets mixed up on the commitment issue.

Some students head into their freshman year with a significant other in tow from their high school days, and on occasion, these relationships are sustainable through college into a happily married life. At other times, college opens the eyes of one of the other members of a couple to new aspects of themselves and the direction of their lives, and it soon becomes obvious that the relationship can't go any further. Most college students, however, enter college with a clean slate, as well as a hope that they'll find companionship, if not love. This includes students like you who value their Catholic faith.

There are a few things to look out for if your hope is to be called to marriage. First, it can be tempting for an overzealous new Catholic college student to place potential partners under an undue level of scrutiny, subjecting them to a Catholic litmus test that no normal Catholic could live up to. Individuals with these kinds of standards can end up crossing someone off their list of possibilities the first time they see them accidentally order a cheeseburger on a Friday in Lent.

Another pitfall for marriage-minded Catholic students is referred to by some Christians as *missionary dating*: the tendency to see the good in someone to whom you're attracted and to date them with the idea that one day you'll eventually turn them into a practicing Catholic. Still another temptation involves idealizing someone who has deep faith and trying to force attraction where attraction does not exist just because you want to marry a good Catholic.

On the other hand, it can also become easy to cross shared values off your list of priorities altogether when smitten by someone you consider to be a candidate as a potential spouse. It's important to approach the search for a spouse with an ear attentive to God's voice rather than your own plan for what you think your life should look like; only then can you allow God to pleasantly surprise you.

And it should be mentioned as well that although God grants us the desires of our hearts, our way forward may be both unknown and unexpected. Pay attention to your desires, but also be open to God's desire for you; for whether you understand the will of God or not, our God loves us and desires that we live a life worthy of the call we have received. Sometimes discerning this call will not arrive neatly overnight. It takes time, openness, and a heart willing to trust in God's will.

Recall a time when you were pleasantly surprised by a sequence of events that did not go according to your own plans.

_____

_____

_____

_____

_____

_____

_____

_____

Of course, there are those God has set apart neither for the vocation to chaste single life as a layperson nor to marriage but to his service in a unique way through the priesthood or religious life. In a world that looks down on celibacy, the first roadblock for someone who might be struggling with this call is often the idea of giving up the chance to have a natural family. In an age in which priests and religious aren't as common as they may have been even fifty years ago, it can seem to be a lonely vocation, at least from an outsider's perspective.

Interestingly enough, however, in survey after survey in which people are asked whether their jobs make them happy, priests consistently end up atop the list, ahead of doctors, lawyers, teachers, and a host of other professions that might be considered fulfilling. As a matter of fact, in December 2011, *Business Insider* ranked clergy Number 1 in its *10 Jobs With the Happiest Workers* survey. If priesthood or religious life is where God has called you, rest assured it will be the most rewarding path you can travel as you seek to grow closer to Christ. If God calls you to religious service, don't waste that golden opportunity to pursue mere worldly success, which is bound to fade.

How Do I Discern My Vocation?

A number of great saints have undertaken the question of how to discern the ways in which God sets out a plan for a person's life. For some people, a vocation to marriage, single life, priesthood, or religious life becomes crystal clear from a young age; for others, it's something that develops over time. For some, there is a distinct *aha!* moment when they realize that they have a religious vocation or that they're supposed to marry the person they're dating. For others, it's better understood as a process, and only by looking back at the patterns of God at work in their lives can they see the direction in which God was leading them all along.

When discerning God's will for our lives, it can be easy to think that we're discerning what God wants us to do for a living or what our career trajectory should look like. These are of course important points to consider, but it's also important to realize that at the most basic level, God's will is the same for all of us: to know, love, and serve him, as the very first lesson of the *Baltimore Catechism* states. If we don't strive to conform ourselves to that primary aspect of the will of God, it will be difficult to discern what God's will is in regard to our vocation.

How would your family react if you told them you were getting married? If you had a call to the priesthood or religious life?

_____

_____

_____

_____

_____

_____

_____

As Saint Francis de Sales tells us, "It sometimes happens that the means of attaining salvation considered *en masse* or in general, are agreeable to our hearts, while they terrify us when considered in detail and in particular" (*Finding God's Will for You*, Sophia Institute Press, 1998). Even for those who may be excited about their call to marriage or a religious vocation, they will encounter challenges and struggles along the way.

There is no easy path to holiness, but the joy you'll receive in the long term will make every complication along the way completely worth it. In his book *Finding God's Will for You*, Saint Francis reminds us that before the rubber truly met the road, Saint Peter verbally expressed his willingness to follow Jesus to his death but abandoned him at the crucifixion once things began to get difficult. Fortunately for Saint Peter, and for us, just because we may succumb to our own human weakness as we stumble down the path toward our vocation, it doesn't mean God can't do something great with us, as he did with Saint Peter, whom he appointed as the first pope.

If you find yourself questioning whether you are being called to a religious vocation as you make your way through college, don't dismiss the question altogether just because you're not sure how the details might play out. There's a reason they call this process discernment. You are trying to hear God's voice rather than that of your own doubts and fears. These days, we may be tempted to think of those who enter seminary or a religious novitiate as people who have already discerned their call, but in actuality, these men and women are enrolling in these formation programs *in order* to discern whether they have a call.

In previous decades it was not uncommon for Catholic families to send multiple sons to seminary just to ensure that if one of them had a vocation to the priesthood, he would have ample opportunity to discern that call. If in the course of your college life you *think* you might be called in this direction, what could it hurt to at least meet with a diocesan vocation director or a representative of a religious order that aligns with your talents and spiritual priorities? Many dioceses and religious orders do a great job of having a presence on college campuses and would be more than happy to answer any questions you may have, so don't be afraid to ask. Just remember, asking questions doesn't mean you're committing to anything.

What clubs, groups, or teams have you committed yourself to in the past year? How did you initially get involved with them?

_____

_____

_____

_____

_____

A committed prayer life is essential to the discernment process, but it's important to maintain a listening ear while engaging in it. It can be all too tempting to try to talk God into whatever plan we already think is best for us, convincing ourselves that he's signed off on our will, rather than being silent and waiting for him to speak to us. God speaks to us in many ways: through Scripture, meditation, the witness of others, nature, our daily lives, and multiple other ways. Similarly, it can be tempting in our prayer lives to approach our vocational dilemma like one might go about solving a math problem or a career-counseling inventory. As it's often been said, God doesn't necessarily call those who are equipped so much as he equips those whom he calls.

If in prayer you discern that God is calling you to a particular vocation, don't live in fear of your own weaknesses, because you have no idea how God might be able to use even those to further the work of his kingdom. Just like married people can be engineers, doctors, teachers, accountants, athletes, and musicians, so priests and religious can come from the same backgrounds and can use those unique skills to benefit the Church in ways that show forth not only their own talents but also the diversity of God's plan to further the kingdom.

In your interactions with peers, family members, teachers/professors, or others, do you tend to be more of a talker or a listener? How does the way you communicate with these people compare to the way you communicate with God in prayer?

_____

_____

_____

_____

_____

Another key to the discernment process is humility. When we were asked as children what we wanted to be when we grew up, we all had our answers: astronauts, athletes, actors, animal trainers, and the like. By the time we get to college, some of us are still on the path toward possibly accomplishing those ends. And yet we all know, for example, wonderful mothers who gave up potentially lucrative careers to stay at home with their children and have zero regrets about their decision. Likewise, if during the course of your college years you find God is calling you to something that doesn't seem to follow what you happen to think is "the plan," you'll need humility to accept that. It's important to know, though, what humility actually means. Humility isn't thinking you're dumb when you're actually smart or thinking you're terrible at something when you're exceptional at it. That's false humility, and it's lying about yourself just as surely as inflated egotism is. True humility consists in understanding who you are in relation to God, not just warts and all, but talents and all as well. Telling the truth to yourself and God about who you are can help open the channels of communication and better facilitate the discernment process.

What's the one vocation you think you couldn't follow in a million years? Why don't you think you could do it? How would you respond if it started to become clear that God was calling you to that vocation?

_____

_____

_____

_____

_____

_____

_____

It may be to your advantage to seek out a spiritual director while at college, if you don't already have one. One of the better ways to go about this is by approaching a priest involved in campus ministry or at the parish where you attend Mass. You could also ask a campus minister for a list of spiritual directors, because in our day, not all spiritual directors are priests. If the priest or campus minister is unable to aid in your spiritual direction, then they will no doubt be able to help you find someone who can.

Spiritual direction is something altogether different than the sacrament of reconciliation or emotional counseling, although both may be involved in the process. Most spiritual directors try to take into account your talents, struggles, background, and difficulties, and take you from one level of spiritual growth to the next based on these. Having a spiritual director can be extremely helpful in the vocational discernment process, because you may be too close to your thoughts and emotions to know what God is asking of you in a particular situation or to what vocation God may be calling you. Think of it as a second opinion.

In discussing your questions with a spiritual director, you may recognize some aspect of God's call that was right in front of your face all along but needed to be pointed out by someone else for you to see it. But spiritual direction also guides your spiritual life. Spiritual directors will ask you about your prayer life, school life, and friendships to help you achieve balance in your daily living.

Whatever your vocation, you are meant to show forth in it the love between Christ and his Church. As Saint Paul tells us in Ephesians 5:31–32, "'For this reason a man will leave his father and mother and be joined to his wife, and the two will become one flesh.' This is a great mystery, but I am applying it to Christ and the church." If your call is to marry, you will be living the most obvious form of what Saint Paul is talking about here; if you are a priest who acts in the person of Christ, you are a spouse to his Church and illustrate Saint Paul's analogy in that way. Religious sisters, so often referred to as "brides of Christ," are also an image of the Church. No matter what life God has called you to, you are to serve so as to illustrate God's relationship to his people, which we see here imperfectly, but will see perfectly when

Jesus the bridegroom welcomes us at the end of time. It is a challenging responsibility, but one that should be a great source of excitement for all of us who seek to do God's will.

ALUMNI DIRECTORY
Saint Maria Faustina Kowalska
(1905–1938; born in Russia and died in Poland)

As a young Catholic in twentieth-century Poland, Saint Faustina was born into a low estate, attending only three years of school before having to drop out and work in her teenage years as a maid to help support her family. When she felt the call to religious life, she applied to several orders but was repeatedly rejected.

At age nineteen, while attending a dance with her sister, she had a vision of the suffering Jesus asking her to enter the convent immediately. That night, without even asking her parents, she packed her bags and boarded a train to Warsaw, where she knew nobody, and began staying in the home of an area woman who provided her with room and board while she applied to religious life. Unfortunately, Faustina continued to get negative responses from the orders to which she applied, being told that someone of her financial state would be a burden to the community. Finally, she applied to the Sisters of Our Lady of Mercy, where the Mother Superior agreed to let her join, provided she could raise the money to pay for her habit.

Working for nearly a full year, and periodically depositing her wages at the convent, Faustina was finally able to start her novitiate in 1926. Her life as a nun was to be a short one, lasting only a decade before she died of tuberculosis, but during that time she received multiple visions of Jesus, who told her to spread the message of his Divine Mercy.

Faustina recorded these visions in her diary, but because of her lack of education, they were badly misspelled and a grammatical mess. However, in 1965 the Archbishop of Krakow, Karol Wojtyla (who would go on to become Pope John Paul II), commissioned a translation of her works and took on the personal mission of spreading her visions to the world. It was under Pope John Paul II that Maria Faustina Kowalska was eventually declared a saint, and it was also under him that Divine Mercy Sunday was placed on the liturgical calendar, scheduled to fall one week after Easter Sunday.

Perhaps you're familiar with the image that reflects Saint Faustina's vision of our merciful Lord: Jesus, hand outstretched, dressed in white, with a pale ray and a red ray coming forth from his chest. The words underneath this image should serve as a motto for all attempting to discern their vocation: Jesus, I trust in you.

MEMORY VERSE

"We know that all things work together for good for those who love God, who are called according to his purpose. For those whom he foreknew he also predestined to be conformed to the image of his Son, in order that he might be the firstborn within a large family. And those whom he predestined he also called; and those whom he called he also justified; and those whom he justified he also glorified" (Romans 8:28–30).

CATECHISM OF THE CATHOLIC CHURCH
Love

"Love is the fundamental and innate vocation of every human being" (*CCC* 2392).

EXTRA CREDIT
Practical Steps Toward Realizing the Call

- Contact a married couple, a priest, and a member of a religious order. Ask each of them individually how they discerned that they were being called to their state of life. Was it something that came to them early in life or later? What surprised them about the way God called them? What would they have done differently along the way had they known the kind of life to which God was calling them?

- Through your school's campus ministry, ask for a directory of religious orders in proximity to your college. Look into the history and function of some of them, including their charisms, and see if there is an opportunity to volunteer in any of their apostolic work.

- Most orders will not accept candidates until they are debt free. If outstanding student loans and other expenses are keeping you from religious or clerical life, contact either the Mater Ecclesiae Fund for Vocations (fundforvocations.org) or the Laboure Society (labouresociety.org). These two organizations provide resources to help pay off the student loans of those who are trying to pursue their vocations.

- If you find yourself at a crossroads, try this tip recommended by a friend who is a diocesan vocation director. Block out an hour of time for Eucharistic Adoration, and spend the first half hour imagining what life might be like as a married person, with all the joys and challenges associated with it. Spend the second half hour imagining what life might be like as a priest or religious. At the end of that hour, reflect on which one brings you the most peace. Take notes while you reflect.

SUGGESTED READING

- *Tuning In to God's Call* by Andrew Carl Wisdom, OP, and Christine Kiley, ASCJ. This book is set up almost as a retreat, walking you through the discernment process so as to help you open your heart to God's call for your life. Should you marry the person to whom you're attracted? Is God calling you to the priesthood or religious life, the diaconate, or perhaps a rigorous single life where only the dedicated celibate can tread? The daily devotional setup of this resource can help you look at the path to which God has called you in a progressive set of reflections.

- *Finding God's Will For You* by Saint Francis de Sales (Sophia Institute Press, 1988). Saint Francis takes an interesting approach to discerning God's will—one that might seem strange until you get the hang of it. He doesn't look at vocational discernment like many of us might look at a math problem. Rather, he relates it to an ongoing spiritual journey where change doesn't always mean contradiction, and the revelation of what you're supposed to do with your life in a strange way can reveal how you've been prepared all along for the path to which God has called you.

- *What's Your Decision? How to Make Choices with Confidence and Clarity* by J. Michael Sparough, SJ; Jim Manney; and Tim Hipskind, SJ. The path of discernment discovered by Saint Ignatius has proven helpful to a number of Catholics who are desperate to find the path to which God is calling them. Using the Spiritual Exercises of Saint Ignatius, the authors look at the elements of discernment through the eyes of Saint Ignatius and provide practical ways to explore the experiences God has given you so that you can determine the vocational path toward which you're being called.

PRAYER

As you offer your life to Christ in the vocation to which he has called you, consider making this morning offering from the Apostleship of Prayer as soon as you turn off your alarm each day:

"O Jesus, through the Immaculate Heart of Mary, I offer You my prayers, works, joys, and sufferings of this day in union with the Holy Sacrifice of the Mass throughout the world. I offer them for all the intentions of Your Sacred Heart: the salvation of souls, reparation for sin, and the reunion of all Christians. I offer them for the intentions of our bishops and of all Apostles of Prayer, and in particular for those recommended by our Holy Father this month."

Our Father, who art in heaven,
hallowed be thy name;
thy kingdom come,
thy will be done
on earth as it is in heaven.
Give us this day our daily bread,
and forgive us our trespasses,
as we forgive those who trespass against us;
and lead us not into temptation,
but deliver us from evil.

Hail Mary, full of grace,
The Lord is with thee.
Blessed art thou among women,
And blessed is the fruit of thy womb, Jesus.
Holy Mary, mother of God,
Pray for us sinners, now and at the hour of our death.

Glory be to the Father, and to the Son,
And to the Holy Spirit.
As it was in the beginning,
Is now and ever shall be,
World without end. Amen.

Social Media: Getting Connected or Holding You Back?

Finally, beloved, whatever is true, whatever is honorable, whatever is just, whatever is pure, whatever is pleasing, whatever is commendable, if there is any excellence and if there is anything worthy of praise, think about these things.

PHILIPPIANS 4:8

Every successive incoming class of college freshmen enters a slightly (or sometimes even drastically) more technologically advanced situation than the one before it. Accessibility to research material, and even professors and tutors, has increased dramatically through the evolution of social media. Add to that the various ways in which video chat technology has made it easier to connect with off-campus relatives and the fact that most of your fellow students will own a laptop, a smartphone, a tablet, or all of the above, and you might begin to realize that we live in the age of the "connected campus" now more than ever.

What technologies are available to you now that weren't available at the end of your eighth-grade year? Have they had an impact on you as a person? If so, how?

_____

_____

_____

_____

_____

We've spoken before about the use of social media from a time-management perspective, but in this chapter, we'll try to dig into some of the ways we use the media, both negatively and positively, so as to better appreciate the gift of connectedness that God has allowed us to develop, and use it to the most beneficial end during the college experience without allowing it to warp our sense of what connectedness should mean.

Why It's Important to Take This Chapter Seriously

We've probably all heard of the potential drawbacks of the exponential spread of social media—how it can be distracting, time consuming, and keep us from tasks we should be doing. However, we have to be aware of the more subtle dangers associated with social media as well, such as how it might cause us to treat people differently, both in online and in-person interactions.

It's all too easy to fall into the trap of texting people rather than talking with them and messaging multiple parties online while never giving any substantial attention to any of the people we're actually trying to message. And we can't neglect to address the way in which social-media use can negatively affect our prayer lives as we reduce our sense of communication to digital exchanges that have little or no connection to our lived everyday realities.

That said, social media can positively enhance the college experience from a spiritual perspective in tons of ways. One of the most obvious examples of this is in terms of connectedness with family members off campus. In the days before smartphones, or even cell phones, one of the only ways to immediately connect with parents was through a land-line telephone, often one that had to be shared with a roommate. Now technology has advanced to the state where mobile video chat is often available on many hand-held devices. For homesick students who feel totally at sea in their first weeks on campus, this can be an extremely comforting way to connect with family.

Through what form of social communication did your parents prefer to communicate with you during your high school years? What form of communication did you prefer when you wanted to communicate with them?

_____

_____

_____

_____

_____

For your own sake, as well as the sake of your family, it's important that you make it a point to connect with family members while you're away from home. It can be tempting to think that a new life on campus means you can leave the old trappings of child-parent relationships behind. But remember that you're not totally on your own yet, and as much as your parents might try to stay out of your business, they really do care what's going on in your life. While you're using social media to connect with new people on campus as well as old friends from high school, don't neglect to drop a line every once in a while to your family.

It may be helpful here to define what we mean by social media. Generally understood, social media is any form of technology that allows you to interact remotely with others. That includes everything from phones to social-networking sites and blogs to multiplayer online gaming, file sharing, and much more. Social media are tools, and just like chain saws, sledgehammers and nail guns, they can be used for good purposes or bad ones. It can be a daunting task to go step-by-step through the ways each of these specific media should be employed by you as a Catholic college student, but a few guiding principles should apply to the way you approach them so that you master the use of social media so that it doesn't end up mastering you.

Are you the master of your use of social media, or does social media tend to master you?

_____

_____

_____

_____

_____

All in Moderation

As Saint Paul says in 1 Corinthians 6:12, "'All things are lawful for me,' but not all things are beneficial. 'All things are lawful for me,' but I will not be dominated by anything."

The Church doesn't discourage the use of new media; rather, we are encouraged and instructed to use it. For example, in one of the recent Spiderman films, Spiderman's Uncle Ben quotes the philosopher Voltaire and reminds us that "with great power comes great responsibility." God has allowed us to create the media we have so that we can be better connected to one another as a human family and better share in the knowledge of both the Creator and the world God created.

The temptation will always exist to abuse any tool, and with social-media use, this temptation is particularly strong when it comes to time management. It can be easy to lie to ourselves and say we're diligently researching a project, when at the same time we also have our social-networking profile and a few active chats going on in the background. It will take more discipline than ever to focus your efforts on one thing at a time while studying for college-level courses, even as friends of yours who don't feel the need to study try to communicate with you via social media. When you find yourself in that situation, do yourself a favor and close out every window except the ones related to your work. You'll get things done faster and have more time for social interaction that you can actually enjoy.

Also, you don't have to spend every second of your college career plugged into some kind of device. It's OK to turn off the MP3 player, the TV, and the laptop every once and a while and just go for a walk without tripping over your feet the whole time because you're trying to text simultaneously. You've moved into a new environment, so do a little real-world exploring that doesn't involve technology. Otherwise, you may miss some of the more interesting aspects of your new campus home.

List three places you'd like to explore further in and around campus.

_____

_____

_____

College is a time in which many people dig into personal questions of philosophy and religion in a way they weren't able to do while living under their parents' roof. And while conversations among students about the biggest questions in life can take place in coffeehouses, bars, dorm rooms, and the campus cafeteria, they often spill over into the online world where things people couldn't think of in the moment in person can be edited and retyped before being submitted to the discussion.

In fact, many people feel far more confident talking about issues of philosophy and religion in a social-media context than in a face-to-face setting. You can pretty much count on the fact that in the course of some of these conversations, your Catholic understanding of morality, truth, and pretty much everything else is going to be challenged in the process.

There are a few reactions that people of all faith backgrounds tend to have when challenges to their belief system arise. Sometimes a confronted Catholic can avoid the topic altogether and shrink back into a safer community, walling themselves off from any discussion that entertains ideas that might be contrary to Church teaching. For those who don't yet feel confident enough about their faith to publicly defend it, this may be a perfectly reasonable option, at least until that confidence is developed. On the other end of the spectrum lies the reaction of some ardent Catholics who fight fire with fire, answering nasty questions with nasty answers. This approach often tends to further embitter the person with the opposing worldview against the Church. This kind of conversation always generates more heat than light and is made all the more possible by the anonymity of the Internet. You can't get in a bar fight if you're not in an actual bar.

The best way, however, to engage questions or even attacks on your Catholic faith (which will inevitably arise in both social media as well as face-to-face conversations) is to consistently employ the theological virtue of charity. It can be easy to think of the person on the other side of an online conversation more like the bad guy in a video game to be destroyed for fun rather than a human being made in the image and likeness of God just like you are. Charity means you don't say anything online to someone that you wouldn't feel comfortable saying to them in person.

Think of the last debate you got involved in over the Internet. How comfortable would you be saying the things you typed in that discussion if the person with whom you were debating was sitting across the table from you?

If charity means thinking of each person with whom you interact online as made in God's image, then it also means recognizing the dignity of each person in terms of why the person believes what he or she believes. This attitude enables you to personalize your discussions in a way that answers the actual questions the person is asking. For instance, if you're discussing the validity of what Catholics believe about the Virgin Mary with a Protestant Christian, it makes sense to explain that belief based on Scripture, since both Catholics and Protestants believe in the validity of Scripture. If you're talking to an atheist about sexual morality, however, it makes no sense to base your argument on Scripture, because they believe in the infallible moral authority of the Bible about as much as you believe in the infallible moral authority of Star Wars. For that discussion, an exploration of natural law and the existence of objective truth will probably be far more fruitful for all involved parties.

Recall a time when a belief central to your identity as a Catholic was questioned. How did you respond? Were you proud of the way you reacted, or do you wish you had handled the conversation differently?

Remember, just because you have the ability to search for something on the Internet doesn't mean you actually know everything. If you become stuck in a controversial conversation, have the humility to admit you don't know the answer to the question, but also have the charity to look up the answer or wrestle with the question. Much of our faith is mystery, and if we are to be just in our arguments, we also have to search for truth through prayer and study. If the person you're conversing with is really seeking the truth rather than just trying to make you look like a fool, they'll appreciate the humility you show.

Another great guiding principle when it comes to the use of social media as a college student is the intermittent employment of silence. Pope Benedict XVI made this the theme of his 2012 World Communication Day message: "Silence is an integral element of communication.... By remaining silent we allow the other person to speak, to express him or herself; and we avoid being tied simply to our own words and ideas without them being adequately tested. In this way, space is created for mutual listening, and deeper human relationships become possible."

If you live in a noisy dorm, silence is hard enough to come by, but in addition to external noise, it's also necessary to quiet the internal noise that can be the product of media overload. How often have you gone to Mass and found your mind wandering to sports-related scenarios, reality-television plot lines, annoying songs that have gotten stuck in your head, clever ways to respond to something you saw on the Internet, or a thousand other things that have nothing to do with the Mass?

Silence often makes us uncomfortable, because in an age that moves as fast as ours, we feel like we're wasting time if we're not actively doing something or consuming some form of media. We're so focused on what we ought to do that we often lose sight of who we ought to be. Many people who can't seem to achieve silence in private prayer give up their efforts altogether and pursue what they perceive to be more practical problem-solving avenues.

Where do you go when you want to get some quiet time? Why this place in particular? If you don't have a place yet, what might be somewhere to go to clear your head of the noise imposed by your surroundings?

_____

_____

_____

_____

As with anything, silence requires practice. If you can only clear your mind for one minute of prayer today, you can either use that as an excuse to abandon prayer because you don't think it works for you or you can steel your will and try for two minutes tomorrow. It will always be easier to check your e-mail or text someone than it will be to communicate with God in prayer unless you start to prioritize social interaction with him the way you prioritize social interaction with the rest of your network.

Spiritual fitness requires the same kind of diligence as physical fitness. Just as gym exercises help you strengthen your bodily muscles, so spiritual exercises strengthen your spiritual muscles. We've spoken in previous chapters about the importance of vocational discernment during the college years, and cultivating silence is a crucial aspect of opening yourself to hear God's voice. This is not only about his ultimate plan for your life, but about God's will at work in every individual moment.

What's holding you back from periodic silence? What's one practical step you can take to overcome that obstacle?

_____

_____

_____

_____

One of the great things about the development of social media is the number of tools now available for Catholics in the form of apps and web resources. For instance, when it comes to those inevitable coffeehouse discussions where your beliefs are challenged, catholic .com (the web portal for *Catholic Answers*) has hundreds of well-written and succinct articles to help you defend your Catholic faith, which you can access easily through a smartphone or digital tablet. There are also tons of great Catholic smartphone and tablet apps that enable you to pray the Liturgy of the Hours daily, get reflections on the day's Mass readings, or listen to podcasts or streaming Catholic content from dozens of great websites. There's even an app developed by the Fellowship of Catholic University Students (FOCUS) that provides a host of articles, webcasts, and interactive content tailored specifically to the needs of Catholic college students.

Depending on how you approach it, social media can be your best friend or your worst enemy. You'll find that many of your fellow students approach social media uncritically and you probably won't be surprised when the person who plays video games all night or texts constantly instead of studying isn't on campus anymore after the first semester. It's up to you to make sure that your own stewardship of social media balances work, prayer, and leisure in a way that enhances your college experience rather than detracting from it.

Reflect on which form of media takes up most of your free time, whether it's social networking, playing video games, or something else that tends to pull you away from studying or other important responsibilities. What are some ways that you could better balance your time management in regard to this particular form of social media?

_____

_____

_____

_____

ALUMNI DIRECTORY
Saint Maximillian Kolbe (1894–1941; born in Poland and died in Auschwitz concentration camp)

Most people know Saint Maximillian as the priest who offered his own life in exchange for the life of a married man with young children who was condemned to death in the Nazi prison camp at Auschwitz. However compelling the end of his life might be, his missionary spirit through the course of his life deserves attention as well.

Born into a Polish Catholic family at the turn of the twentieth century, Maximillian had a vision of the Virgin Mary in which he was offered two crowns: a red one, representing martyrdom, and a white one, representing purity. He accepted both, and would attain both as his life unfolded. He joined the Conventual Franciscans at age sixteen and used his God-given intelligence to study math, physics, theology, and philosophy. He fell in love with learning and passed that enthusiasm on to his students.

However, he didn't feel that his desire to spread the Gospel should be confined to the classroom alone. He went on to embrace the popular media of the day, which at that time was the established medium of daily newspapers and the budding medium of Catholic radio. He even founded his own station. Kolbe saw that in the face of growing threats to the Church through Fascism, secularism, and Nazism, the best offense was a good defense. So he defended Catholicism against its detractors in peaceful and charitable ways. When he was arrested for his criticism of Nazi occupiers in his native Poland, he surrendered willingly, as Jesus did, answering paganism with peace rather than a sword.

His witness serves as a challenge to all of us whose blood boils every time we hear our faith attacked. Kolbe's example reminds us to persist in the truth and remain charitable against all odds.

MEMORY VERSE

"If I speak in human and angelic tongues but do not have love, I am a resounding gong or a clashing cymbal. And if I have the gift of prophecy and comprehend all mysteries and all knowledge; if I have all faith so as to move mountains but do not have love, I am nothing" (1 Corinthians 13:1–2, NAB).

CATECHISM OF THE CATHOLIC CHURCH
Golden Rule

"Charity is the theological virtue by which we love God above all things for his own sake, and our neighbor as ourselves for the love of God" (*CCC* 1822).

EXTRA CREDIT
Practical Steps in Relation to Social Media

- Make it a point to call home at least once a week, if only for five minutes, to check in with family members, be they parents, grandparents, or siblings. Make sure your parents also know how to contact you via phone, e-mail, or your social network in case they have important news to share.

- Find one or more regularly updated Catholic websites or Catholic apps that can be used on a daily basis, and make it a point to incorporate them into your schedule. If you're using prayer-related apps, try to set alarms on your computer or mobile device to remind you to stop for prayer at a certain time of the day when you know you can set distractions aside for a few minutes.

- Designate one hour per week to unplug from all media. Depending on your schedule and project due dates, the hour may rotate. It may be helpful to schedule it early in the week so that if you have to put it off temporarily for other responsibilities, you will still have time left in the week that you can set aside as a media-free zone. Sunday, our day of rest, may be a good time for this.

SUGGESTED READING

- *Prayer in the Digital Age* by Matt Swaim. Swaim digs into the perils of cultural engagement faced by denizens of the digital age and uses the insights of the Doctors of the Church in regard to their own cultural challenges to pray. Read this book and see how they might apply to contemporary culture in regard to social media.

- *How to Defend the Faith Without Raising Your Voice* by Austen Ivereigh. A lay Catholic from Great Britain, Ivereigh sought out how to respond to the inevitable attacks on Catholicism that would take place in his home country as a result of Pope Benedict's 2010 visit to the United Kingdom. With charity and clarity, Ivereigh breaks down the objections of non-Catholics to the Church in a way that can take the heat out of a debate over Catholicism and bring reason and charity to discussions regarding the Church.

- *The Church and New Media* by Brandon Vogt. As editor of this volume, Vogt shows a number of ways in which the Church's approach to interaction via social media can take place, looking at dialogues between Catholics and non-Catholic Christians, dialogues between Catholics and people of other faiths, and dialogues between Catholics and those of no faith at all. He also gives practical voice to the ways in which diocesan administrations are trying to navigate the new mission territory of social communications.

PRAYER BEFORE LOGGING ONTO THE INTERNET
by Fr. John Zuhlsdorf

Almighty and Eternal God, who created us in your image and bade us to seek after all that is good, true and beautiful, especially in the divine person of your only-begotten Son, Our Lord Jesus Christ. Grant, we beseech you, that, through the intercession of Saint Isidore, Bishop and Doctor, during our journeys through the Internet we will direct our hands and eyes only to that which is pleasing to you and treat with charity and patience all those souls whom we encounter. Through Jesus Christ, Our Lord. Amen.

Appendix

Sample Monthly Budget for Catholic College Students

You might find it helpful to create a spreadsheet document using the following criteria so that you can be a good steward of your limited resources as a student. Some of the expenses listed below may be automatically covered by your tuition, or may be paid by your parents. If that's the case, leave the field blank. If this exercise depresses you now, it'll encourage you later if you stick to a budget and keep your finances in check.

INCOME	BUDGETED	ACTUAL
Work		
Family/Gifts		
Stipends/Other		
INCOME TOTAL		
EXPENSES		
Room and Board		
Phone		
Food		
Transportation (this can include car payments, insurance, gas/public-transport fees		
Church/Charitable Giving		
Entertainment		
Miscellaneous		
INCOME MINUS EXPENSES		

About the Authors

Colleen Swaim teaches high school religion and English at Covington Latin School in the Diocese of Covington, Kentucky. The author of *Radiate: More Stories of Daring Teen Saints* (Liguori, 2012) and the best-selling *Ablaze: Stories of Daring Teen Saints* (Liguori, 2011), she spent her undergraduate years studying English at The Catholic University of America in Washington, DC, and earned her MEd in Secondary English Education at Xavier University in Cincinnati, Ohio.

Matt Swaim works at Sacred Heart Radio in Cincinnati, Ohio, and is the producer of "The Son Rise Morning Show," a nationally syndicated program on the EWTN global Catholic radio network. The author of *Prayer in the Digital Age* (Liguori, 2011) and *The Eucharist and the Rosary* (Liguori, 2010), he holds a BS degree in Media Communications (2002) from Asbury University.

Colleen and Matt reside in Cincinnati, Ohio, with their son, Zeke.